TRUTH: A PRIMER

TRUTH: A PRIMER

Frederick F. Schmitt
UNIVERSITY OF ILLINOIS
AT URBANA-CHAMPAIGN

Westview Press
BOULDER • SAN FRANCISCO • OXFORD

Focus Series

Published in 1995 in the United States of America by Westview Press, Inc., 5500 Central Avenue, Boulder, Colorado 80301-2877, and in the United Kingdom by Westview Press, 36 Lonsdale Road, Summertown, Oxford OX2 7EW

A CIP catalog record for this book is available from the Library of Congress.
ISBN 0-8133-2000-3—0-8133-2001-1 (pbk.)

Printed and bound in the United States of America

The paper used in this publication meets the requirements of the American National Standard for Permanence of Paper for Printed Library Materials Z39.48-1984.

10 9 8 7 6 5 4 3 2 1

For

Hugh Chandler

Contents

Preface

This primer is a brisk introduction to philosophical thinking about truth. It covers the chief historically important theories of truth: the correspondence theory, pragmatism, coherentism, and deflationism. It also reviews some closely related topics: realism and idealism, absolutism and relativism, and the implications of the nature of knowledge for truth. My primary interest in the book is to convey the gist of classical issues, arguments, and theories of truth. In the course of the book, I tie the issues and theories together as facets of an underlying concern—whether truth involves a relation to human thinkers. It is a concern of the first importance, in league with other concerns about the relativity of the world to human thought. I attempt to bring out how these concerns are manifested in classical theories of truth.

For each theory, I have gone immediately to the heart of the matter and treated only the most central points. I have aimed to present the issues and views in an intuitive way, focusing on philosophical rather than historical or interpretive points. I have not, however, avoided the deepest philosophical questions. This occasionally makes for rough going, but I prefer exposure to the real thing to the protectionism that is currently the fashion in introductory texts.

In treating the issues in an intuitive way, and in presenting the historically important theories as competing theories of the same thing, truth, I have had to disentangle the theories from the philosophical systems in which they were originally embedded. I have also had to drop the dialectical settings that distinguish these approaches to truth. I am aware that such a treatment may mislead and even deprive a theory of its point, but I believe that, for introductory purposes, the clarity and simplicity gained by an issue-oriented approach is worth the risk.

Talk about, and against, truth has recently gained popularity outside of philosophy. It is now common among literary theorists, sociologists of science, anthropologists, educational theorists, and others to deride classical theories of truth, especially the correspondence theory, and even to oppose the very aim of true belief. I don't suppose people who declaim against such ancient virtues as truth and consistency ought (if they are consistent!) to care much about the accuracy of their claims, but for those who do, this book may serve as a measure of the accuracy of recent discourse about classical theories of truth.

The book emerged from my need for a very short text on truth to supplement the primary readings for my undergraduate epistemology course. Ideally, students entering an epistemology course would come equipped with a mental map of the terrain of truth. In my experience, however, students tend to know little about classical theories of truth. I originally wrote the book to fill the gap.

In the writing, the book developed into a work that can sustain the truth segment of an undergraduate metaphysics, philosophy of language, or semantics course. It might also serve as a supplementary text for undergraduate or graduate courses in areas that do not strictly cover the topic of truth, but require some background in it—not only epistemology, but also philosophy of science, metaphysics, and philosophy of logic. The book assumes no knowledge of logic or philosophy of language. Nevertheless, there should be points of interest to specialists on these subjects.

As will be evident, I have been influenced greatly by Hartry Field's important work on truth, especially his paper "The Deflationary Conception of Truth" (1986). Other recent works by which I have been influenced, and with which I substantially agree, include Gerald Vision's *Modern Anti-Realism and Manufactured Truth* (1988) and Ralph Walker's *The Coherence Theory of Truth* (1989).

Some readers will be aware that until very recently there was no available introduction to the topic of truth. Richard Kirkham's *Theories of Truth* (1992) has now appeared. There will be no need for another systematic introduction to the topic for a very long time to come, and this primer makes no attempt to compete with Kirkham's impressive achievement. The point of a primer is to introduce the subject directly and without pomp and circumstance, and that is what I have attempted here. One cannot do better than Kirkham for a comprehensive discussion of the topic.

To forestall disappointment, let me list some issues that for brevity I will have to omit here: whether the bearers of truth-values are propositions, sentences, or statements (I will generally assume that they are propositions, but I do not believe that much hangs on this); the relation between truth, assertion, reference, meaning, and information; "eternal" truths and indexicals; degrees of truth and quantity of information; whether "true" is a predicate of sentences or a sentential operator; the semantical paradoxes such as the liar paradox; local realism vs. idealism; truth-theoretic theories of meaning; justification-theoretic theories of truth and meaning; and Wittgensteinian theories of truth and meaning. The reader will find these and other issues discussed not only in Kirkham but in Michael Devitt and Kim Sterelny's excellent *Language and Reality* (1989).

I would like to thank Hugh Chandler, Matthew Davidson, Art Melnick, Jim Spellman, and an anonymous referee for helpful comments. I must thank Keith Lehrer, one of our series editors, and Spencer Carr of Westview for making this volume possible.

Frederick F. Schmitt

Introduction

Philosophers have always taken an interest in the nature of truth, both for its own sake and for its broad implications in each of the main branches of philosophy—metaphysics, epistemology, ethics, and logic. This book explores the nature of truth by evaluating the chief historically important theories of truth: the correspondence theory, deflationism, pragmatism, and the coherence theory. The correspondence theory is ancient and was endorsed, explicitly or implicitly, by nearly every philosopher who had much to say about truth before the year 1800—philosophers as diverse as Plato, Aristotle, Spinoza, Hume, and Kant. Pragmatism and the coherence theory, in contrast, are inventions of the nineteenth century. It took twentieth-century minds to conceive of deflationism.

These theories share the assumption that truth has a common nature—is one and the same thing for all topics to which it applies. The theories then set about the task of capturing this nature. To do so, they propose necessary and sufficient conditions for a truth-bearer's being true—i.e., for a proposition, sentence, or statement to be true. These conditions may be intended to reveal the meaning of "true," or they may be intended as expressing a necessary correlation between truth and some other property—theorists of truth do not often distinguish these tasks. Beyond the assumption that truth has a common nature, and perhaps an additional platitude or two about truth, there is little agreement.

Correspondence theorists, pragmatists, and coherentists hold that truth is a genuine property of propositions or a relation between propositions and other things. Deflationists, however, deny that there is anything more to truth than what is involved in the linguistic use of the predicate "true." Theorists arrive at these views from quite different theoretical directions. Correspondence theorists begin with the role of the notion of truth in the explanation of behavior. Pragmatists are concerned to explain the usefulness of true belief. Coherentists hold out the hope of making truth knowable. And deflationists wish to explain the role of "true" in linguistic acts like assenting to a proposition. The historically important theories of truth in fact differ so broadly in orientation that it is difficult to bring them into contact with each other. One might even wonder whether there is any one thing, truth, that the various theories of truth attempt to capture. Evidently the theories must have a single target, if they are genuine competitors. Yet it proves difficult to characterize truth in a fashion that is neutral between the theories.

We might seek to join the theories by attempting a list of platitudes about truth to which all parties would agree. One author (Wright 1992, 33-70) has even offered such a list as a minimal *theory* of truth. But it is doubtful that there is any list of platitudes rich enough to count as completely characterizing truth, yet weak enough to satisfy all disputants. Another way to get started in our discussion of the historically important theories is to treat each theory as a separate venture, embedded in a philosophical program to which it makes a distinctive contribution. There are two obstacles to this approach. One is that a theory of truth like the correspondence theory, or even pragmatism or coherentism, has been employed in diverse philosophical programs. There is no one program to which it makes a contribution. The other obstacle is that this approach is bound to lose sight of the competition between the theories of truth recognized and intended by their proponents.

How, then, should we proceed? I suggest that we proceed on the assumption that theories of truth attempt to capture a unique ordinary notion of truth. Each theory begins with an intuitive idea about the nature of truth so conceived. In the case of the correspondence theory, the intuitive idea is that truth is a relation of correspondence between a proposition and the way the world is. In the case of pragmatism, the idea is that truth is essentially related to useful belief. For the coherence theory, the idea is that truth is essentially related to justified belief. After developing these intuitive ideas, we may then search for natural arguments for and objections to the views.

Though these theories of truth arrive at their accounts of truth from quite different angles, there is a fundamental matter to which all theories are party: they all pronounce on whether truth involves a deep relation to thinkers. All the historically important theories of truth allow that in one way or another truth involves a relation to thinkers. This is so not only for pragmatism and coherentism but for deflationism and the correspondence theory as well. For example, on the correspondence theory, a belief is true just in case it corresponds to some fact. Clearly, this relation of correspondence entails a relation between a believer and the corresponding fact, if only because a believer is related in some standard way to his or her beliefs. The historically important theories of truth, then, share the assumption that truth involves a relation to thinkers. Indeed, they hold that this is so by virtue of the meaning of "true" or by the very nature of truth.

There are, however, various ways in which truth might involve a relation to believers, some deeper and more interesting than others. Theories of truth diverge in just how truth involves a relation to believers. The precise way in which truth involves such a relation is, in my view, the central point of contention between classical theories of truth. It will accordingly be our primary focus in this book.

One issue between classical theories of truth is whether truth involves a relation to the *ascriber* of truth. The correspondence theory denies this, whereas deflationism and certain versions of pragmatism and coherentism affirm it. A second issue is whether truth must in some way be relativized to a subject or system of beliefs or to a truth "user." That issue separates relativism (including relativist versions of pragmatism and coherentism) from absolutism (including absolutist versions of the correspondence theory and deflationism). A third issue divides epistemic theories of truth (like coherentism) from nonepistemic theories: does truth (again, by virtue of the meaning of "true" or the nature of truth) in some way *depend* on the mind? These issues constitute the central point of contention between the historically important theories of truth. They will play a crucial role in the arguments for and objections to the various theories of truth, and we will deal repeatedly with them from various angles.

Before we proceed to the historically important theories of truth, however, it will help to grasp two disputes that are intimately related to the issues we have just canvassed. One is the dispute between realism and idealism. This dispute turns on a matter parallel to the issue between epistemic and nonepistemic theories of truth: whether the existence of objects depends essentially on human beings. We will take this up in Chapter 1. The other dispute we will need to address is the dispute between absolutism and relativism about truth, the topic of Chapter 2. Our conclusions about these matters will favor certain theories of truth over others. In subsequent chapters, we will take up the historically important theories, and in Chapter 7, we will consider the bearing of the topic of knowledge on the nature of truth.

Chapter One

Realism and Idealism

Realists and idealists debate the nature of existence. They agree well enough on which things exist—mountains, houses, people, planets, and perhaps electrons, governments, and elections—but they differ over what it is for things to exist. Realists maintain that objects exist independently of human thought, whereas idealists, for their part, insist on the mind-dependence of objects. Though the issue originated in ancient Greek philosophy (Groark 1990), a thorough development of realism and idealism had to await the stark contrast between mind and body first drawn by Descartes in the seventeenth century (Burnyeat 1982). In the following century, Berkeley, Leibniz, Kant, and Hegel developed rich versions of idealism. The issue remains a central concern in contemporary philosophy.

At first blush, the *ontological* question whether objects are mind-dependent may seem irrelevant to the *semantical* issue of the nature of truth. (I will use "semantical" mainly in its broader sense—having to do with mental or linguistic representation—rather than its narrower sense of having to do with meaning.) Certainly the question of the mind-dependence of objects *parallels* the question with which, as I claimed in the introduction, classical theories of truth are concerned—the question whether truth involves a relation to thinkers. But one might wonder whether there is more to the connection between the questions than a mere parallel. I will postpone a close look at the connection till Section VI below. Here it suffices to summarize the relevance of the realism-idealism debate: a choice between the historically important theories of truth turns on a judgment of the plausibility of idealism. At the same time, the issue between realists and idealists has great interest in its own right.

I. Realism and Idealism

We may define "realism" and "idealism" in this way:

> *Realism*: All objects are wholly mind-independent.
> *Idealism*: All objects are at least partly mind-dependent.

Realists see objects as existing independently from human minds. An intuitive case for realism takes off from an observation. It cannot be that existing things depend on our minds. For we withhold an ascription of existence to something whenever we discover that it depends on the mind. Thus we withhold ascribing existence to Hamlet when we learn that he is a character in a play. The realist generalizes this observation to a view of the nature of existence: no objects, or existing things, are products of the mind; all objects are wholly mind-independent.

Idealists, in contrast, launch their case from some agreeable points about knowledge and representation. We must have access to existing things in order to know them, and we must of course be able to represent existing things in order to refer to them. The idealist then proposes that we can have access to or represent only those objects that are in some way constituted by the mind. Accordingly, all objects depend for their existence on the mind.

Before we develop these lines of thought, I think it would be helpful to make some clarifying remarks about the above definitions of realism and idealism.

(1) For convenience, I have chosen to focus on *objects* rather than on facts or on the whole world. Realism and idealism could be expressed as views about the mind-dependence of facts or of the world, but the questions that arise on these alternative formulations closely parallel the questions we will consider about objects, so I see no need to complicate the discussion by entertaining these alternative formulations.

(2) "Object" may be taken as subsuming all existing things. I wish to avoid embroiling our discussion of realism and idealism in two other important issues that are historically related to it. One is the question whether there are things other than objects—e.g., states of affairs, events, or properties. The name "realism" is sometimes given to the view that there are properties distinct from objects. This issue—which, in its farther Platonic reaches, concerns how abstract or conceptual the world is—cuts across the realism-idealism divide with which we are occupied. Another issue is whether there are *merely* possible objects—whether there are objects that do not in fact exist. Realism here is the view that there are such objects. This issue, too, is orthogonal to our own.

(3) I have formulated the issue between realism and idealism in terms of *all* objects regardless of their kind. That is, I have defined realism and idealism as *global* realism and *global* idealism. There are, however, *local* versions of realism and idealism as well, versions that apply only to objects of one kind or another. Realists and idealists can dispute about physical bodies, numbers, or moral values. What matters for our purposes, however, is the global dispute. For we are concerned with the global nature of truth, and it is the global issue between realists and idealists that is relevant to the global nature of truth.

(4) Note that the realism-idealism contrast is between objects being *wholly* mind-independent and their being *at least partly* mind-dependent. One might worry that this way of making the contrast burdens the realist with an unreasonably strong view and thus puts realism at a disadvantage. This is a legitimate worry. However, I am prepared to defend the strong version of realism defined here, on certain interpretations of "mind-independent." I do not regard the view as overly strong. I have chosen to focus on these versions of realism and idealism because the best arguments for idealism, if successful, establish only that objects are partly mind-dependent, not that they are wholly so, while the best objections to idealism tell against partial mind-dependence and not merely against total dependence. Thus, the case for realism, to the extent that it succeeds, establishes strong realism, while the case for idealism is a case for weak idealism.

(5) Note, too, that realism and idealism, so defined, do not exhaust the possible positions one might take. Logically speaking, there is room for a middle view on which some objects are wholly mind-independent and others are at least partly mind-dependent. An intermediate view would combine a *local* realism with a *local* idealism. Although such a view might at first blush seem agreeable, I am inclined to doubt whether it is viable. For realism and idealism attempt to capture what it is for an object to exist, and I believe that existence is such a simple matter that its nature will be uniform for all objects. If this is true, then either realism or idealism will hold globally. A middle position is ruled out. But we need not consider further whether such a position is correct. As I have already mentioned, what matters for our purposes is the plausibility of global idealism. So the plausibility of global idealism is the proper target of our investigation. On the other hand, and by the same token, it does not matter for our purposes whether global realism turns out to be true or instead an intermediate position. As it happens, I believe that a global

realism is defensible, so I will examine global realism as the alternative to global idealism.

(6) Realism and idealism have been defined in terms of dependence on the mind. It is unavoidable to ask: whose mind? One answer would be: anyone's. That is, on idealism, an object exists if it is constituted by some mind or other. Of course that answer puts considerable pressure on the notion of "constitution" that appears in the definition of mind-dependency, since we do not think that figments of the demented count as existent. If idealism is to be tenable, "constitution" had better be defined in such a way as to avoid allowing that just anything conjured up by some mind or other counts as existent. An alternative version of idealism would hold that whether an object exists is in some way *relative* to a mind. According to this version of idealism, an object exists, relative to a mind, if it is constituted by that mind. I confess, though, that I have no idea what it means to say that an object exists relative to a mind. The idea lacks the intelligibility of another relativist idea, one to be taken up in the next chapter, that propositions are true or false only relative to subjects.

For the time being, the foregoing comments will suffice to direct our attention to a certain issue. To make further progress in comprehending this issue, we must say what mind-dependence is supposed to be. I have already suggested that it is *constitution* by the mind. Just what such constitution comes to, and why the debate turns on constitution by the *mind*, must emerge from whatever intuitive case can be made for realism and idealism, to which I now turn.

II. Arguments for Realism

As I have suggested, realists begin their study with an observation. We withdraw an ascription of existence to Hamlet when we discover him to be a character in a play (assuming we have no reason to believe that he was a genuine historical personage). We withdraw our ascription of existence when we learn that an item is fictional. Presumably the reason such a withdrawal is appropriate is that the item is (partly) constituted by the mind in a certain way: the item has its features in virtue (in part) of the mind's representation of the thing. From this simple observation, the realist launches the general view that objects or existing things are mind-independent in the sense that they are not constituted by the mind even in part. Realism, so understood, contrasts with an idealism on which objects are partly constituted by the mind in virtue of being represented by it. The realist's observation suggests that idealism is at odds with how we go about ascribing existence to things. Indeed, idealism seems at odds even with what we *mean* when we say that something exists. We may label the realism and idealism that emerge from the realist's observation *r-realism* and *r-idealism*—"r" for representation.

To comprehend what is at issue between r-realists and r-idealists, it may help to contrast the dispute between them with another dispute, a dispute over the *counterfactual* dependence of objects on the mind. On a counterfactual interpretation of the issue, realists and idealists clash over whether objects are in part *counterfactually dependent* on the mind, idealists holding that they are and realists holding that they are not.

To understand counterfactual dependency, it will help to know what a *counterfactual conditional sentence* is. It is a sentence of the form "If it were the case that p, then it would be the case that q"—for a shorthand example, "If I were taller, I would play more basketball." This is called a counterfactual conditional sentence because it is a conditional sentence (i.e., a sentence of the form "If A, then B") and the conditional imposes a contrary-to-fact condition, a condition that does not obtain (in the given example, the condition of being taller than I actually am). A *counterfactual dependence* of an object x on another object *y* is a dependence that can be defined by the counterfactual conditional sentence:

If *y* didn't exist, *x* wouldn't exist.

By instantiation, the counterfactual dependence of an object *x* on the mind may be defined by the counterfactual conditional sentence:

If minds did not exist, *x* would not exist

(equivalently, *x* would not exist unless minds existed). We are now in a position to understand the counterfactual interpretation of the issue between realism and idealism. On this interpretation, realism claims that there are *no* objects that counterfactually depend on the mind. Idealism, by contrast, declares that no objects would exist unless minds existed.

From the perspective of one who wishes to be a realist, the trouble with this counterfactual dependency interpretation of realism is that it makes realism patently false. For there are obviously many objects that are counterfactually mind-dependent. No one will want to deny that artifacts like automobiles and paintings exist and are objects in just the sense in which mountains and trees are objects. Yet the former are counterfactually mind-dependent while the latter are not. More interesting and perhaps controversial examples of counterfactually mind-dependent objects include minds, social groups, and social institutions. And there are other counterfactually mind-dependent things that plausibly exist, though they are not ordinarily said to be objects. Examples include such properties as gender and stage of life (childhood, adulthood). It is obvious that these would not exist without minds. This is true even if gender and stage of life are not, as some aver, "socially constructed" in the sense that their existence and nature depend entirely on being understood in the way that they are.

Whatever one thinks of these examples, everyone must agree that there are *some* counterfactually mind-dependent things. Realists must grant that artifacts like automobiles and paintings are as existent as any natural objects—as rocks and birds. Thus, interpreting mind-dependence as counterfactual mind-dependence makes realism a view that can be accepted only by those willing to embrace a heroic ontological distinction between natural and artificial objects. That distinction cannot be sustained.

Clearly, then, realism can be credible only if mind-dependence is conceived as involving something more than counterfactual mind-dependence. One way to understand realism is as claiming that objects are mind-independent in the sense that they are not even in part *constituted by the mind*. But even this does not give a fine enough point to realism. To be plausible, realism must be understood as involving something more than mere *constitution by the mind*. For automobiles are arguably *partly* constituted by the mind (though equally arguably partly not constituted by the mind). What it is to be an automobile is to have a certain function in human life, and this involves being treated by human beings in a certain way; hence it involves human beings having certain thoughts and attitudes toward automobiles.

On what interpretation of mind-dependence and constitution by the mind, then, might realism be credible? One such interpretation was already suggested in passing at the outset of this section: identify mind-dependence with *constitution by the mind in virtue of being represented by it*. The realist, now an r-realist on our definition, holds that no objects are constituted by the mind in virtue of being represented by it. Such a realism no longer denies that objects are counterfactually mind-dependent. It is obvious that automobiles are counterfactually mind-dependent. But it is far from obvious that automobiles are (even partly) constituted by the mind in virtue of being represented by it. So realism no longer falls afoul of the obvious. Automobiles, as the realist may admit, are mind-dependent and constituted by the mind because being an automobile is having a certain function in human life, and having that function entails, among other things, being recognized as an automobile. Such recognition, in turn, involves representation—in this case, the representation of something as an automobile. But it is not as if this representation (in part) makes the thing an automobile, still less makes the automobile exist. The representation is a condition of the automobile's having a function but it does not give rise in any sense to the existence of an automobile. The situation regarding automobiles is quite unlike that regarding Hamlet. Whatever existence Hamlet may have—and of course the realist would and the idealist may deny that he has any—would have to be endowed by the representation of Hamlet in the play *Hamlet*. Hamlet exists in virtue of being represented in the play *Hamlet*. His features are created by the play's representing them. The features of an automobile, however, are not created by our representing them.

Revisiting now the starting point of realism, we can see that the r-realism which we are now entertaining does not merely say that objects are mind-independent in the sense that they are not constituted even in part by the mind. For this is not enough to regard them as fictional. An automobile is partly constituted by the mind, and gender may be wholly constituted by the mind. Rather, r-realism holds that things count as fictional when they are partly constituted by the mind *in virtue of being represented* by it. The r-realist may plausibly deny that automobiles or gender are even partly constituted by the mind in virtue of being represented by it. Rather, these things are constituted by the mind in the sense that they exist because people interact with objects (chunks of metal and, increasingly, plastic in the case of automobiles, and human beings in the case of gender) in a certain way. So understood, r-realism is far from patently false, as it would be if interpreted in terms of mere counterfactual mind-dependence or constitution by the mind.

We now have a more pointed understanding of what is at issue in the debate between r-realists and r-idealists, and we may proceed to the relative merits of these views. Let us begin with the support for r-realism. One source of support is of course what I have been calling the starting point of r-realism, but before we examine this initial motivation more closely, let us look first at some other sources of support for r-realism.

The traditional arguments for realism support versions of *local* realism rather than the global realism with which we are engaged here. They attempt to show that certain mind-independent objects *actually exist*. Realism as we have defined it—global realism—does not entail the claim that any such objects actually exist; rather, it entails that any objects that do exist are mind-independent. Nevertheless, arguments for local realisms, if fruitful, provide indirect support for global realism, for two reasons. One is that global realism does entail local realism about any object that is assumed to exist: if we assume that an object exists, then global realism entails that it is mind-independent, and this is equivalent to local realism about that object. A second reason that arguments for local realism also support global realism is that global realism could be supported by arguing, for each type of existing thing, that things of that type are mind-independent. Global realism might even be supported by an *inductive* argument: local realism is true of this or that type of existing thing; hence by induction, it is true of all types of existing things. Thus, the arguments for local realisms are quite pertinent to our evaluation of global realism.

There are perhaps two major arguments for local realism that indirectly support global realism:

The Causal Argument

This is a popular form of argument, the most famous example of which is René Descartes's argument for the existence of mind-independent physical bodies in the *Meditations on First Philosophy* VI (1985). Descartes's argument begins with the observation that sensory experience is more or less independent of our will. It is worth distinguishing two ways in which this is so. Our visual impressions of bodies—say, of an elm—are both *constant* and *intermittent.* My impression of the elm occurs intermittently, depending on whether I am in the vicinity of the elm, my eyes are open and turned toward the tree, and so on. But many features of the impression, at least many, if not all, of those in virtue of which the impression represents the elm, are constant with each intermittent stage of the impression: all these stages share the features in virtue of which the elm is represented as having a certain color, shape, texture, etc. Our will—our intentions and decisions about what we perceive—cannot explain the constancy and intermittency of our impressions, since our impressions remain the same or vary in a way quite independent of what we will. Nor are there any other mental states to which we can plausibly ascribe the constancy and intermittency of our impressions. Consequently, our impressions are most likely produced by something other than our mental states—namely, by mind-independent bodies. This argument may be augmented by the observation that there is a coincidence—sometimes called *consilience* (Whewell 1989, 154-155, 159, 163-164)—among the features of impressions of various sensory modalities: e.g., certain features in the visual mode are correlated with certain features in the auditory mode. This is another sort of constancy best explained by mind-independent bodies. The general form of argument is that we must postulate mind-independent objects of a certain kind in order to explain certain features of experience that cannot be explained by mental states alone.

The causal argument for realism about bodies falls short of the mark. For even if the argument showed that mental states do not *cause* the features of experience, it would not follow that they do not *constitute* the bodies that cause these features. Perhaps the constancy and intermittency of experience are caused by bodies distinct from these experiences. But nothing in the argument shows that these bodies do not exist in virtue of being constituted by experiences and other mental states—e.g., by being represented by them. We represent these bodies as having certain features—as existing continuously rather than intermittently, and as causing experiences. The r-idealist may hold out for the view that bodies exist and have these properties in virtue of these very representations, the representations they (in part) cause. More generally, idealists may hold out for the view that bodies are constituted by the mind.

One might object to this way of defending r-idealism on the ground that the proposed combination of idealism and the causation of bodies by representations is circular: how can the objects constituted by representations cause the representations that constitute them? Despite appearances, there is no circularity here. It is only if we confuse constitution by the mind with causation by the mind that the objection appears to have force. There is more to say about whether idealism suffers from a circularity, but I will postpone the matter till Section III.

One might, however, question the idealist response for another reason: how can bodies persisting at variance with experiences and mental representations of those very bodies be constituted by these representations? But the idealist may observe that there is no logical obstacle to a situation in which a represented object could obey conditions of persistence quite different from the persistence conditions of the mental states that represent them. This point too, though strictly correct, raises a problem we will have to take up later. For now, we must concede that the causal argument for realism is by itself inconclusive.

The Pragmatic Argument

Another popular argument for local realism is that mind-independent objects best explain the success of certain practices. This argument is most often used to secure *scientific* realism—the view that the theoretical entities postulated by science have a mind-independent existence. On this argument, we must postulate, say, mind-independent electrons to explain our success in using the electron microscope to develop an effective vaccine for disease. How could the electron microscope enable us to develop a vaccine unless the entities postulated by the theory that explains how the machine works really exist—namely, mind-independent electrons?

Plausible as it may seem, this pragmatic argument suffers from a problem similar to the one that afflicts the causal argument. Even if the argument establishes that electrons *exist*, there is nothing here to secure their *mind-independent* existence. The existence of electrons is enough to explain our success in developing vaccines. Of course, if it could be assumed that our developing vaccines is mind-independent, then we might need to postulate mind-independent electrons to explain our success. But such an assumption would obviously beg the question in favor of realism. We may, therefore, set aside the pragmatic argument for local realism as inadequate.

Neither the causal argument nor the pragmatic argument for local realism can be made to support global realism—any kind of global realism, whether global r-realism or another version of global realism. Let us return, then, to the starting point of r-realism and ask whether this starting point can yield a successful argument for the view.

The starting-point of r-realism, the reader may recall, is a simple observation—that we withdraw an ascription of existence to a thing when we discover it to be constituted by the mind in the sense that it has its features in virtue (in part) of representations in the mind. This observation clearly holds for *fictions conjured by the imagination*: when we discover that something we have called Pegasus has its features merely because of a representation in imagination—a representation in Greek mythology—we are no longer willing to say that it exists. Of course we may, if we wish, still speak of Pegasus as "existing in the imagination." But by this we do not literally mean that Pegasus exists; we mean only that we *represent* Pegasus in our imagination. Thus, the observation certainly applies to fictions conjured by the imagination.

But it also holds generally of things that have their features in virtue of being represented. For example, it holds of *creatures of intellectual conception*. If a friend shows me a room empty but for a chair and coffee mug and says, "There are three items in this room: a chair, a coffee mug, and a chug," I have a right to feel cheated when it turns out that a chug is not some hidden object that I have been unable to detect but simply the aggregate of the chair and the mug—a creature of my friend's power of conception. And I feel cheated not because the chug is composed of objects already apparent, the chair and the mug. I would not feel cheated if shown what appeared to be diverse objects that, when put together in the right way, turned out to be a garlic press—something that I would readily concede is an object and does exist. Rather, I feel cheated because a chug is a product of conception. It has its features partly in virtue of a representation in conception—presumably, a mental aggregation of the chair and mug. It is therefore not an object; it does not exist at all. In short, neither fictions of the imagination nor creatures of intellectual conception are plausibly said to exist. And the reason they are not plausibly said to exist is that they have their features (in part) in virtue of representations of the mind. Thus, objects exist only if they do not have their features even in part in virtue of representations of the mind. In other words, r-realism is correct.

How compelling is this argument for r-realism? I see two ways for the r-idealist to challenge the argument. One way is to claim that r-idealism already possesses the resources to distinguish fictions of the imagination or creatures of conception from existent objects. This will be so if, on r-idealism, existent objects are constituted by the mind in such a way as to allow this distinction. The r-idealist may claim that objects are so constituted that we imagine Pegasus and conceive things like chugs, and at the same time, there are garlic presses consisting of assorted parts, and the existing objects include the aggregated parts of garlic presses but not Pegasus and chugs.

We can expect the r-realist to reply to this idealist objection to the argument by denying that on r-idealism garlic presses would turn out not to exist, since they are after all constituted by the mind. Of course, the r-realist will say, we can imagine or conceive of a world like our own, in which there is a fundamental ontological difference between Pegasus and garlic presses. But if the world we imagine or conceive of has its features in virtue of being imagined or conceived, this world and the things in it are fictions of the imagination or creatures of conception and do not exist. The r-idealist may retort that the distinction the r-idealist can make between existing objects and fictions of the imagination (or creatures of conception) exhausts the intuition behind the argument for r-realism, so that nothing more needs to be said to capture this distinction than what the r-idealist can say.

This debate is tough to call, but I am inclined to side with the r-realist here. For there is an effective reply to the r-idealist's objection to the r-realist's argument. That objection depends on an untenable distinction between empirical and transcendental idealism. But we will have to postpone discussing the r-realist reply to the objection until we can properly introduce and evaluate this distinction.

There is, however, a second way for the r-idealist to object to the argument for r-realism. The r-idealist may deny that the argument succeeds in showing that objects exist only if they are wholly mind-independent, as the r-realist requires. Rather, the argument establishes at most that objects exist only if they are *not* wholly mind-dependent—a position consistent with a moderate r-idealism, since r-idealism requires only that objects are not wholly mind-independent. The argument establishes at most this much, according to this second objection, because, although it is plausible that we withdraw an ascription of existence when we discover a thing to be wholly constituted by the mind, it is implausible that we would do so were we to discover it to be only *partly* constituted by the mind. To illustrate the point with the example of the garlic press, the r-idealist might insist that this example precisely favors a moderate idealism. The r-realist's argument ascribes existence to the garlic press, since the garlic press is not wholly constituted by the mind. Yet this object is partly constituted by conception. For something has the feature of being a garlic press in part because of how we conceive of it (as an object with a certain function, to press garlic) and in part as well because of how we use it. The r-realist's argument, then, does not make being constituted in part by the mind a bar to existence. Thus, it does not establish r-realism or rule out r-idealism.

Is this a convincing response to the argument for r-realism? In fact, in introducing r-realism, we characterized the view in a way that deflects this response. For we made r-realism the view that objects do not have their features, even in part, in virtue of representations in the mind. So understood, r-realism does not entail that objects may not exist only if conceived in a certain way. It does not follow from the fact that a thing exists only if conceived in a certain way that it has its features *in virtue of* a representation in the mind. Thus, the r-realist may concede that what it is to be a garlic press is to be a thing that is intended to be used in a certain way (just as what it is to be an automobile or a hammer is to be a thing intended to be used in a certain way). The r-realist may allow that something is a garlic press only if it is conceived in a certain way—in whatever way is required by such intended use. R-realism leaves room for the plausible claim that something is a garlic press only if people conceive of (or would conceive of) it as a garlic press. What the r-realist must deny is that a garlic press is therefore partly constituted by such a conception or that it has its features in virtue in part of representations in the mind.

To clarify the point, we may note that it is natural enough to say that a garlic press has its features (and in particular the feature of being a garlic press) in virtue of the representation of the object as a garlic press. One might take this to favor the r-idealist's response. But talk of having features in virtue of a representation can be interpreted in two ways. In one sense of this phrase, it is true that a garlic press has its features in virtue of a representation: something is a garlic press only if people intend it to be one, and the intention involves a representation. It is a *necessary condition* of something's being a garlic press that it be represented as one. But as we have already seen, this is not the idea of having features in virtue of a representation that the r-realist has in mind. "In virtue of" is not to be understood merely as indicating a necessary condition. Rather, to say that a thing has features in virtue in part of a representation is to say that the representation (in conjunction with other conditions) *creates* these features *by* representing something (in the typical case, by representing the features themselves).

Some contrasting examples may reveal the r-realist's meaning here. The paradigm of something that has its features in virtue in part of representations in the mind is a fiction conjured by the imagination. Hamlet has his features (in this case, wholly) in virtue of a representation (or set of representations) in Shakespeare's play *Hamlet*, in the sense that the play creates these features *by* representing them. This is what the r-realist has in mind in speaking of a thing's having its features in virtue of a representation. The r-realist wishes to deny that Hamlet and other things that have their features in this way—creation by representation—exist. To take a contrasting case (albeit an example of something that is not, intuitively speaking, an object but rather an action), my promise to meet you for dinner entails my intention to meet you for dinner, hence entails a representation in my mind. My intention is, in tandem with my gestures and certain social practices, a sufficient condition of my promising to meet you for dinner. It might be said that my promise exists and has its features in virtue in part of my intention. It might even plausibly be said that the intention (in part) creates the features of the promise. But it would not be agreeable to say that my intention creates the features of the promise merely *by representing them*. Thus, for the r-realist, my promise differs vitally from Hamlet: unlike Hamlet my promise may be said to exist.

If this claim of difference between Hamlet and my promise is intelligible, as I think it is, then the r-idealist response to the argument for r-realism misses the force of the argument. The response fastens on a reading of "mind-independence" not intended by the r-realist. The garlic press is wholly mind-independent in the sense that representations do not create its features by representing anything. Thus, the argument for r-realism may still show that objects are wholly mind-independent in the sense that representations do not create their features by representing anything. The r-realist need not flee to the weaker claim that objects must be at least partly mind-independent in this sense but may hold out for the stronger position that objects must be *wholly* mind-independent. The argument for r-realism survives the r-idealist response.

To summarize our findings about r-realism, the standard arguments for local realism turn out not to support global r-realism. Nevertheless, the starting-point of r-realism generates a forceful argument for the view. If r-realism is defensible, as I believe it to be, then there is at least one important sense in which objects are wholly mind-independent: no objects have their features, even in part, in virtue of representations. In this key sense, the existence of objects does not involve any relation to human or other thinkers. That is true of every object in the universe. Here we come down on one side of the central question whether things (in this case objects, rather than truths) involve a relation to thinkers.

III. Arguments for Idealism

Though adopting r-realism precludes embracing r-idealism, it does not preclude adopting other versions of idealism. R-realism excludes the possibility that objects exist in virtue of being represented by the mind, but it does not rule out other forms of constitution by the mind. There are other contrasts between realism and idealism besides that of r-realism and r-idealism. And, from a logical point of view, r-realism could be combined with any of these sorts of idealism. Thus, even after settling for r-realism, we are a long way from the end of the question whether in any important sense the existence of objects involves a relation to thinkers. To make further progress, we will need to understand these other contrasts between realism and idealism. It will help to begin with some natural arguments for idealism.

The Epistemological Argument

Traditionally realism has been rejected on the ground that it makes it impossible to know objects. This is one ground on which the famous eighteenth-century idealist George Berkeley, whose views we will discuss in more detail below, embraced idealism.

We may appreciate the epistemological argument for idealism by considering its most striking version. The argument proceeds this way. Knowledge requires epistemic access to the object of knowledge. But we have epistemic access only to those objects whose existence we can deduce from our experiences having a certain content. Yet we can deduce the existence of an object in this way only if the object is constituted by the mind. Hence, all knowable objects are constituted by the mind. Add now the premise that all objects are knowable, and idealism follows. This argument, if successful, establishes a version of idealism other than r-idealism (namely, as we will see below, identity idealism or phenomenalism).

The success of this version of the epistemological argument depends on whether there is a notion of "epistemic access" weak enough to be intuitively required for knowledge, yet strong enough to require deducibility from experience. The proponent of the argument must walk a tightrope here—no easy assignment. Let us, however, postpone the evaluation of this version of the epistemological argument till Chapter 7. I will offer criticisms there that I take to be effective against the argument. If I may borrow my conclusion from that chapter, we may say that this version of the epistemological argument fails to secure any version of idealism. I believe the same thing is true of the other versions of the argument, some of which we will treat in one way or another in subsequent chapters.

The A Priori Representation Argument

There are two arguments for idealism from the nature of representation. One is an a priori argument (see Putnam 1990 for a variant of this argument). It appeals to the principle that

> if a representation *R* represents an object *x*, then there must be some condition that makes it the case that *R* is a representation of *x* rather than of some *other* object *y*.

According to this principle, there must be some condition in virtue of which *R* represents *x* rather than *y*. If no condition decided in favor of representing *x* over representing *y*, then nothing would make it the case that *R* represents *x*—and so *R* would not represent *x*.

But, the argument continues, if *x* does not exist in virtue of being represented by *R*, then any condition in virtue of which *R* represents *x* must be either an *intrinsic quality* of *R*, or otherwise a *worldly relation* (e.g., a relation of resemblance or a causal relation) between *R* and *x* itself in virtue of which *R* represents *x*. Yet, so the argument goes, neither of these two options is ever satisfied. *R* never represents *x* in virtue of its intrinsic qualities. For the intrinsic qualities of a representation *R* never by themselves make it the case that *R* represents *x* rather than *y*. Perhaps the most venerable account of representation on which the intrinsic quality of the representation makes it the case that it represents *x* is the Aristotelian view that a representation represents in virtue of taking on the *form* of the object represented. But it now seems extremely implausible that mental representations take on the form of the object represented. A mental representation of a raccoon does not take on the form of raccoon (see Cummins 1989, 27-34, for a review of the problems). For it does not in any way resemble a raccoon. Nor does any worldly relation make it the case that *R* represents *x*. For example, a representation does not more closely resemble x than other objects y. A postcard may represent a resort even though its depiction more closely resembles some other scene. And the same is even more obviously true of mental states, which do not plausibly resemble the objects they represent in any interesting way. Thus, it is not in virtue of resemblance that R represents x rather than y. Nor, the argument continues, can we repose any confidence in causal relations as the condition that will decide that a representation represents x rather than y. Any mental state bears causal relations to many objects: my visual impression is caused not only by the magnolia it represents, but by the sun as well. So R does not represent x because of a worldly relation between R and x. In short, there is no alternative to the conclusion that x must exist in virtue of being represented by R. From this, it follows that any object which we represent must exist in virtue of being represented by our representation. It would seem to follow also that any object that we *can* represent must exist in virtue of some representation we can employ. This is not quite r-idealism, until we add the assumption that, for any object, we can represent that object. Once that assumption is granted, r-idealism follows.

Is this a persuasive argument for r-idealism? I will grant the plausible claim that the intrinsic quality of a representation R never by itself determines that R represents x rather than another object y. I will also waive, for purposes of evaluation, the contentious claim that no causal relation can determine that R represents x rather than y. And I will grant, for the sake of argument, the implausible assumption that for any object we can represent that object. What I find least convincing in the argument is its tacit assumption that if x exists in virtue of being represented, then the condition in virtue of which R represents x need be neither an intrinsic quality of R nor a worldly relation between R and x. Why should the constitution of x by the mind exempt R from the requirement that there is some condition, either an intrinsic quality of R or a worldly relation, in virtue of which *R* represents *x*? The answer would have to be that *R*'s constituting *x* is itself a condition in virtue of which *R* represents *x*.

But in truth I can make no sense of this answer. I agree that *R*'s constituting *x* is neither an intrinsic quality of *R* nor a worldly relation to *x*. But if *R*'s constituting *x* is the condition in virtue of which *R* represents *x*, then the idea is that *R* represents *x* *by* constituting it. The trouble with this is that it gets the "by" relation in constitution backwards. For r-idealism is the view that *R* constitutes *x* *by* representing it. But that view is inconsistent with the idea that *R* represents *x* by constituting it, since a "by" relation is antisymmetric (i.e., if *S* does *a* by doing *b*, then it follows that *S* does *not* do *b* by doing *a*). So a representation's constituting an object cannot be a candidate for the target condition in virtue of which the representation represents *x* rather than *y*. Thus, the idealist can have no advantage over the r-realist in this domain. The a priori representation argument cannot succeed.

The Empirical Representation Argument

Turning now to the empirical representation argument, we begin with the platitude, for which the evidence is empirical if anything, that representations serve our purposes. At the same time, objects are individuated—objectively, that is, apart from the way *we* think of their individuation–in roughly the way we represent them to be and have roughly the features we represent them to have. But we would not expect objects to be objectively individuated in a way that it suits our purposes to do, or to have the features that it suits our purposes to recognize, if objects were not *created* by our representations. R-idealism follows.

I will mention one trouble with this argument. The platitude that our representations serve our purposes, though doubtless true to some approximation, does not obviously support r-idealism. It is true that *we* individuate objects in a way that suits our purposes. But why would anyone take this to show that objects as they are *objectively* individuated are created by our representations, as the r-idealist avers? Nothing here rules out the contrary possibility that our way of individuating objects suits our purposes only *because* it matches the way objects are objectively individuated. The argument does not rule out the possibility that our way of individuating objects facilitates our purposes only because this individuation matches the way objects are individuated by nature. The alternative hypothesis that, as we may put it, subjective individuation recapitulates objective individuation, would provide an explanation of why our representations serve our purposes.

I am not suggesting that the r-realist could commandeer such an explanation and bill it as an argument that we individuate objects as nature individuates them, so that objects must be mind-independent. On the contrary, such an argument would beg the question against r-idealism by employing a premise we could only know if we knew realism to be true, or otherwise by employing a form of inference the r-idealist could reject. Rather, I am pointing out that the r-idealist who endorses the empirical argument must rule out such a realist explanation of why our individuation suits our purposes. Until the realist explanation is ruled out, the idealist cannot take for granted that r-idealism offers the best explanation of why our representations suit our purposes. So the r-idealist cannot claim that we would not expect objects to be individuated in a way that suits our purposes if they were not created by our representations. The platitudinous premise does not obviously lead to r-idealism. This objection seems enough to cast significant doubt on the empirical representation argument.

We have canvassed three arguments for idealism. If my objections have been effective, these arguments cut no ice. The epistemological argument and the representation arguments do not support r-idealism or any other sort of idealism. Given that we have a plausible motivation for r-realism and no argument for any kind of idealism, we may conclude at this point that we ought to embrace at least r-realism. Of course this leaves the option of combining r-realism with any of a number of historically important versions of idealism other than r-idealism. I would now like to turn to these versions of idealism.

IV. Versions of Idealism

Here is a short list of historically important versions of idealism that do not entail r-idealism and that may, so far as our argument has gone and so far as logic allows, be combined with r-realism:

Identity Idealism

For the identity idealist, objects depend on the mind in the sense that they are *identical* with collections of mental states. The most famous of the eighteenth-century idealists, George Berkeley (1982), held such a view for bodies.

Identity idealism is to be sharply distinguished from r-idealism. The two views are indeed mutually inconsistent. For an object cannot both be *identical* with a representation and at the same time created by it in virtue of being represented by it. To be identical with a representation is to be that representation. But to be created by a representation in virtue of being represented by it *excludes* being that representation—assuming, what seems plausible, that self-creation is impossible (at least for entities other than God). To hold both identity idealism and r-idealism about an object would be like saying that Hamlet is both identical with certain parts of the play *Hamlet* (which is, remember, a system of representations) *and* a human character created by the play in virtue of being represented by it. That combination of views is incoherent. It would mean, among other things, that certain parts of a system of representation (the play *Hamlet*) were created by that very system of representation in virtue of representing those parts. Presumably, the human character Hamlet, whatever else he may be, is not a representation in the play *Hamlet*.

Despite the incompatibility of identity idealism and r-idealism, Berkeley appears to have conflated the views. He might have been lured here by certain assumptions he made. He assumed, in particular, that the features of bodies represented—e.g., being red—are also features of the ideas that represent them. This identity between the features of bodies and the features of ideas might have tempted Berkeley to combine the view that a body is the collection of ideas that represent it with the view that the body exists in virtue of being represented by these ideas. This temptation, natural though it may be, must be resisted. For even if the features of bodies just are the features of the ideas that represent them, it seems that what makes the body exist must be *either* whatever makes the *idea* exist or else the representation of the body *by* the idea; it cannot be both. If it is the former, we have identity idealism; if the latter, we have r-idealism.

Virtually everyone now agrees that identity idealism is exceedingly implausible. For the properties of bodies are radically different from the properties of ideas. Bodies have mass and travel at a certain velocity; ideas do neither of these things. So bodies can't be ideas. In short, r-idealism is considerably more plausible than identity idealism. Identity idealism is as silly as saying that the human character Hamlet is identical with some of the lines of the play *Hamlet*. R-idealism involves no such absurdity. However, the advantage r-idealism has in credibility over identity idealism is purchased at the price of obscurity: it is by no means clear how a representation could create an object by representing it; it is far from clear what this could even mean.

Phenomenalism

Another view that is sometimes catalogued as a version of idealism is *phenomenalism*. According to this view, talk about objects is really disguised talk about the mind (Ayer 1955). That is, talk about objects is to be analyzed in terms of talk about the mind or ideas. For example, statements about the sun are to be analyzed in terms of statements about mental states alone. On the simplest version of phenomenalism, the phenomenalist offers this analysis of talk about (for example) the sun:

> "The sun is hot" means, "If a subject *S* were to have certain experiences (e.g., as if going outside on a sunny day), then *S* would have certain other experiences (e.g., of heat)."

Here the references to experiences will have to be cashed ultimately in language that does not employ the term "sun" or "sunny" to refer to the sun, and the reference to an arbitrary subject *S* may have to be replaced by references to actual subjects.

Again, phenomenalism is not r-idealism, any more than identity idealism is. For analyzing object-talk in terms of mind-talk does not entail that our representations create objects *by* representing them—or indeed, create them in any way at all. Phenomenalism says only that object-talk is equivalent to mind-talk, not that the mind constitutes objects. By the same token, however, one might deny that phenomenalism is a version of idealism. Indeed, phenomenalism is not strictly speaking an ontological view. It is rather a semantical view—a view about the meaning of object-talk. On the other hand, it would not be implausible to claim that the view can hold only if identity idealism is correct. For one might doubt whether object-talk can be analyzed in terms of mental-state talk unless objects are constituted by the mind. But we need not decide here whether phenomenalism is a genuine version of idealism or whether it entails identity idealism. It will suffice for our purposes to say a word about its plausibility.

Phenomenalism was a popular view in the early part of this century among the Viennese logical positivists and their British and American followers. Subsequently, however, it suffered withering criticism, and it is now universally regarded as mistaken. Perhaps the most evident objection to the view is that it implies that it is *logically inconsistent* (given the meanings of the terms) to claim that objects can exist without minds. To say that objects can exist without minds is on a par with saying that Dirk is a bachelor but he is married—a logical inconsistency given the meaning of "bachelor," i.e., unmarried man. Yet it seems at least logically possible for the sun to be 93 million miles from earth even though there are no minds in the universe. To be sure, there are idealists who would deny that this claim about the sun is *true*. But even if the claim were false, it would hardly seem false on *logical* grounds (or grounds of meaning) alone. Another way to put the objection to phenomenalism is to say that it is most implausible to suppose that the meanings of our terms *by themselves* decide between realism and idealism. One can surely be a realist without abusing the meanings of terms in the English language. Yet that is exactly what phenomenalism denies is possible. This and numerous related objections defeat phenomenalism.

Functional Idealism

Yet a third version of idealism, more attractive than identity idealism or phenomenalism, begins with an observation about artifacts. What it is to be an automobile is to perform a certain function in human life—to serve as a motorized conveyance of a particular kind. In other words, what we may call *functionalism* is true of automobiles. But performing the function of automobiles involves being treated and conceived by human beings in a certain way. For example, something is an automobile only if people think of it as an automobile. Thus, it is claimed, automobiles are partly constituted by the human mind. That is, a local *functional idealism* holds of automobiles.

The idea of *global* functionalism is to generalize to all objects the local functionalism true of artifacts. The resulting version of idealism is *global functional idealism*: *every* object is constituted by the human mind in the way that automobiles are. Not only artifacts, but natural objects—trees and mountains, planets and electrons—are partly constituted by the mind in this way (see Rouse 1987, 69-165, for a functional idealism that pertains to the objects studied by science, especially theoretical entities like electrons).

Is global functional idealism a plausible view? I see two objections. First, it is doubtful that we can generalize functionalism from automobiles to natural objects. Functionalism is quite plausible for artifacts. Artifacts are what they are in virtue of their function in human life and thus (in part) in virtue of the way people think of them. And it is reasonable to infer from this, as the functional idealist does, that artifacts exist in virtue (in part) of the way people think of them. This inference could be questioned, but I am inclined to grant it. Yet despite the applicability of functionalism to artifacts, the view lacks credibility when applied to natural objects. To see this, we need only take note of the fact that it is implausible that natural objects are what they are in virtue (in part) of the way people think of them. Certainly we do not have the reason for saying so that we have in the case of artifacts. The chunk of metal and plastic of which the automobile is composed might still exist even if we did not think of it as a chunk of metal and plastic—or indeed think of it in any way at all. To suppose otherwise is to confuse this chunk with the automobile itself. More generally, the way natural objects are—their status as chunks of metal or as mountains—does not obviously depend on thought in the manner in which artifacts depend on thought. At least one writer has offered semantical arguments for generalizing functionalism from artifacts to natural objects (Rouse 1987, 69-165). I will have to refer the reader elsewhere for criticism of those arguments (Schmitt forthcoming b). Meanwhile, we may rest with the observation that there is little intuitive impetus behind global functionalism. Consequently, there is little reason to embrace global functional idealism.

Second, and more important, functionalism *cannot* be true of all types of objects. Suppose we say, in the sense intended by the functionalist, that something, *x*, is an automobile only if people think of it as an automobile. Then we must be able to identify *x* independently of conceiving of it as an automobile. That is, there must be some *x* we can identify and individuate prior to conceiving of it as having the role of an automobile. But then, our identification and individuation of *x* cannot be in terms of the role assigned automobiles. We must be able to identify *x* in some other way—e.g., by referring to it under the description "a chunk of metal and plastic." (This is not to say that for any type to which *x* belongs, we must be able to identify and individuate *x* independently of conceiving of it as belonging to that type. For example, it might be that we cannot identify *x* independently of conceiving of it as an object. But for types that are understood as roles, it is surely the case that objects filling those roles are individuated in a manner prior to the roles.)

Now, the global functionalist might reply that the identification of *x* is to be understood in turn in terms of the roles of chunks of metal and plastic in human life. But if so, these must in turn be identified in terms of some further *y* not identified in terms of the role assigned chunks of metal and plastic. Yet it is hard to see how this regress could go on forever. An infinite or circular regress of roles would fail to identify or individuate the objects. This is not to deny that roles in human society might be interdependent in such a way that any particular role must be specified in tandem with all others. It is only to say that characterizing any object in terms of such an interdependent network of roles would require a prior identification and individuation of the objects that take up the roles. Consequently, functionalism cannot hold for all objects. And similarly, functional idealism cannot hold globally. Global functional idealism is mistaken.

Projectivism

A final view that might be classified as a version of idealism is *projectivism*. It is a view inspired by David Hume's treatment of causal necessity, bodies, personal identity, and other matters (see Stroud 1978 for an interpretation of Hume as a projectivist, and Blackburn 1984 for a modern version of projectivism). On this view, we project our thoughts onto the world, treating the world, cognitively, *as if* the objects of our thoughts existed unconstituted by the mind.

Though it is tempting to regard projectivism as a version of idealism, the view turns out, on close inspection, to clash with idealism. For it does not say that existing objects are constituted by the mind. The projectivist's projection by the mind is not the idealist's constitution by the mind. On the contrary, things projected by the mind do not even exist. The spirit of projectivism is thus just the opposite of that of idealism. For the point of projectivism is to explain the appearance of real objects of a certain kind without admitting that there are any objects of that kind. The trick is to say that the objects are merely projected onto the world. But this projection is just what the idealist would call constitution by the mind. When objects are projected, they do not exist, according to the projectivist. But according to the idealist, when objects are constituted by the mind, they exist. Thus the projectivist and the idealist flatly contradict one another. Projectivism does not similarly contradict global realism, since realism says only that no objects are constituted by the mind, not that there are, in any given domain, objects that are not constituted by the mind. Projectivism about a domain and global realism are mutually consistent.

Is projectivism a tenable view? Whatever its merits applied *locally*—e.g., to numbers, geometrical figures, or moral values—a *global* version of the view is untenable. Global projectivism would entail that no objects exist—an absurdity. Thus, we may confidently reject global projectivism.

We have reviewed several arguments for idealism. We have taken a peek at sundry versions of idealism—r-idealism, identity idealism, phenomenalism, functional idealism, and projectivism. I have urged that the argument for r-realism undercuts r-idealism. We should prefer r-realism to r-idealism. And although other idealist views are consistent with r-realism, they face problems at home. There are good reasons to shun all the versions we have seen. But these reasons for rejecting the various versions of idealism so far fall short of a fully *general* objection to idealism. It is time, then, to ask whether any such objection may be found.

V. Objections to Idealism

I believe there are two convincing general objections to idealism, objections that undercut all versions of the view.

The Regress Objection

One general objection is that idealism is incoherent. For it leads to the conclusion that minds must either constitute themselves or else be constituted by yet further minds, generating an infinite regress of constitutings. But it is hard to swallow either of these options. It is hard to see how a mind could constitute itself. How could something make its own existence, even in a noncausal sense of "make"? And it is equally hard to see how there could be an infinite regress of constitutings. How could there be a chain of constitutings that never terminates in a mind existing prior to the chain? These alternatives are boggling however we understand "constituting."

To bring out the absurdity of idealism more starkly, take identity idealism as an example. On this view, all objects are constituted by the mind because they are identical with ideas. Now, the identity idealist might say that minds can, on this view, constitute themselves because they are, after all, self identical. But this would be a lame version of idealism about minds. For on this view minds constitute themselves only in the sense in which everything constitutes itself: everything is self-identical. Thus, it is hard to see how the identity idealist can say that minds constitute themselves. Can the identity idealist take the alternative approach of admitting a regress of constitutings? This would seem to be equally ruled out. For according to identity idealism, constituting is a matter of identity. Yet a regress of identities is impossible: a regress of constitutings must involve an infinity of *distinct* entities, but identities hold only between objects that are identical.

The incoherence of idealism is even more evident on r-idealism. For on this view, the idea that the mind constitutes itself is analogous to a situation in which a play creates itself by containing a representation of its own existence. But in this situation the play that does the constituting is itself nothing but a representation in the play. And this is surely incoherent. The idea of a regress of constitutings is equally incoherent—a play constituted by a further play, constituted by a yet further play, and so on. So the regress objection applies to r-idealism just as forcefully as to identity idealism. The objection seems to apply to idealism quite generally. The culprit—the assumption that gives rise to the absurdity—is simply global idealism itself: that everything is constituted by the mind.

Can the idealist reply persuasively to the regress objection? I do not see how a *global* idealist can avert the objection. Idealism is coherent, in my view, only when restricted to objects other than minds. In other words, the idealist must adopt a local realism about minds and a local idealism about bodies and other objects. This is indeed the approach taken by classical idealists like Leibniz (1951) and Berkeley (1982), who treat minds as mind-independent and bodies as constituted by minds. These philosophers never faced the regress objection because they had no temptation to treat the mind as constituted by anything. Berkeley, for instance, holds that for bodies, to be is to be perceived, whereas for minds, to be is to perceive.

While such a restricted idealism averts the regress objection and restores coherence to idealism, it nevertheless faces two grave problems:

(1) It can work only if the idealist can tender a principled reason for restricting idealism to nonminds. What is needed is a dualist ontology—one that distinguishes minds ontologically from bodies. And this dualist ontology must reveal why constitution by the mind is required for bodies but not minds.

Yet it is doubtful that the idealist will be able to find any reason for adopting a dualist ontology of this kind. For one thing, the standard arguments for idealism—the epistemological and representation arguments—would not lead to a dualist ontology of this kind, even if they worked. For the mind is itself something we know and represent. Consequently, whatever idealism flows from the requirements of knowledge and representation per se must apply to minds as well as to bodies. These arguments are just as convincing (or lame) applied to minds as they are applied to bodies. It is not possible to argue for idealism about bodies by appeal to the general nature of knowledge and representation and at the same time to deny idealism about minds. In the absence of the standard arguments for idealism, it is unclear whether the idealist will be able to find a principled reason for restricting idealism to nonminds.

(2) The second problem with the restrictive approach is this. The regress objection seems to show that idealism *cannot* apply to every object that is not a mind. For if minds constitute bodies, they are able to do so because they are themselves sustained by supporting objects and conditions—the brain, oxygen, the earth, and so on. Yet it is just as hard to see how the mind could constitute the supporting objects as to see how it could constitute itself. Consequently, restricted idealism must exempt these objects as well as the mind. But these supporting objects are, ontologically, a motley bunch. It is hard to believe that they mark a profound ontological rift. Thus, restricted idealism lacks credibility.

In my view, these objections to restricted idealism render it unpalatable. At the same time, restricted idealism is the idealist's only way to fend off the regress objection. Thus, in the end, the regress objection makes a compelling case not only against global idealism, but also against the restricted version designed to stem the regress.

The Counterfactual Mindlessness Objection

The second general objection to idealism is that it runs afoul of some of our most powerful and stable intuitions about objects. We think that trilobites would have existed even if no minds (at least, no human minds) had ever existed. This is something we believe on a number of grounds, the most obvious of which is that trilobites *did* exist before there were any minds—a point we take to be massively supported by scientific evidence: the fossil record, geological stratification, carbon dating, etc. Yet idealism entails that no objects would have existed if no minds had existed, since all objects are constituted by minds. Idealism therefore contradicts deep-seated intuitions about objects. This objection applies not only against global idealism but even against idealism restricted to bodies.

To rebut this objection, the idealist must somehow have it both ways. The idealist can mollify common sense only by allowing that

> (C) Trilobites would have existed even if no minds had existed.

At the same time, the idealist can sustain opposition to realism only by insisting that (C) is not true—indeed, that trilobites would not have existed if no minds had existed. The idealist is stuck, then, making contradictory claims. Moreover, in making these apparently contradictory claims, the idealist must be using words with the same meaning to refer to the same objects. For the realist may reasonably insist that in the claim of realism words have their common meaning. Indeed, the realist may plausibly insist that realism *is* the commonsense claim with which the idealist wishes to agree (and disagree). The counterfactual mindlessness objection thus makes an impressive case against idealism.

Can the idealist rebut the counterfactual mindlessness objection by having it both ways, allowing (C) and at the same time maintaining that trilobites would not have existed if no minds had existed? The only way to do both of these things, it seems, is to distinguish two levels at which (C) is assigned a truth-value and to argue that (C) may be consistently assigned contrary truth-values at the different levels. The proposal here is that we view objects from two vantages. From one vantage, we view them as they have been constituted by the mind. So viewed, (C) is true: trilobites would have existed even if no minds had existed. From this *first-order* vantage, the commonsense claim holds. But there is another vantage as well. We may also view objects from the perspective of the conditions in which the mind constitutes objects. And so viewed, (C) is not true—indeed, trilobites would not have existed if no minds had existed. From this *second-order* vantage, the commonsense claim does not hold. (See Kant 1965 and Putnam 1990 for versions of this two-tier strategy for dealing with the counterfactual mindlessness objection.)

Let us label the proposal that there are two vantages from which to view objects—the first- and second-order vantages—*transcendental idealism*. Because transcendental idealism allows that (C) is true from the first-order vantage, it accommodates a *kind* of realism. This realism is variously called *empirical* or *internal* realism. It counts as realism because it makes objects mind-independent from the first-order vantage. (C) is true from this vantage. At the same time, transcendental idealism makes objects mind-dependent from the second-order vantage. Thus in a way it rejects realism and embraces idealism. It rejects *transcendental, external*, or *metaphysical* realism. One who wishes to maintain realism as a view inconsistent with transcendental idealism must either maintain that (C) is true from the second-order vantage or, otherwise, deny that there is any real distinction between first-order and second-order vantages and maintain that (C) is uniquely true. We may call the view that (C) is true from the second-order vantage *transcendental* realism. And we may call the view that there is no distinction between first-order and second-order vantages, and that (C) is uniquely true, *plain* realism.

I am inclined to think that the realist who wishes to oppose idealism is best off responding to transcendental idealism by defending *plain* realism rather than transcendental realism. (*Empirical* realism is of course not an option for this realist, since it is not opposed to transcendental idealism, but part and parcel of it.) In favor of plain realism, and against transcendental idealism, is the point that the distinction between first-order and second-order vantages makes doubtful sense. This is a point that tells against transcendental realism as well as transcendental idealism. If there is no distinction between the two vantages, then common sense will have us accept (C) as uniquely true, and plain realism will follow.

Now, the point of distinguishing first-order and second-order vantages is to allow us to assign (C) different truth-values in such a way as to maintain both common sense ((C) is true) and idealism ((C) is false). It is not easy to see, however, how (C) can, with one and the same meaning, be true from one vantage and false from another. Talk of vantages here does not render this possibility salient. From different vantages, a sentence can *appear* both true and false, but can it *be* both true and false? Different vantages are just that—vantages on the same thing. Certainly, from different vantages on a thing one can perceive different but *consistent* features of the thing, and one can perceive features that *appear* to be inconsistent. But one cannot perceive *inconsistent* features. Since being true and being false are inconsistent features of a sentence with one meaning, one cannot, from different vantages, perceive that a sentence is true as well as false. (The relativist about truth will deny this—a matter we will have to postpone until the next chapter.) To be sure, there are plausible examples in which the same *sentence* is both true and false. "Rodriguez is tall" is true if we are speaking against a comparison class of baseball players; but the same sentence is false against a comparison class of basketball players. But to say that the same *sentence* is both true and false is not to say that the same *proposition*—the sentence, given a unique meaning—is both true and false. "Rodriguez is tall" apparently means different things in the two instances. Once the meaning of the sentence is specified (by specifying the comparison class), the truth-value must, it seems, be unique.

Now, the transcendental idealist may respond by admitting that in general the truth-value of a sentence is unique once the sentence has been assigned a meaning. But the transcendental idealist may at the same time insist that there are certain kinds of sentences that are exceptions to this rule, one of these kinds being counterfactual conditional sentences. Consider this example (cited by Walker 1989, 30):

> If Bizet and Verdi had been compatriots, Bizet would have been Italian.

When asked whether this is true or false, we are stymied. If we evaluate the sentence by holding Verdi's nationality fixed and varying Bizet's, then we will say it is true. If, on the other hand, we hold Bizet's nationality fixed and vary Verdi's, we will say that it is false. But we are at a loss as to whether to evaluate it in one way rather than the other, and so at a loss as to whether to say that it is true or false. We could either say that it is true or that it is false, depending on which way we choose to evaluate it.

Similarly, the transcendental idealist may say, if we evaluate (C) by holding fixed the features of the world *as it is constituted*, then we will say that (C) is true. But if we evaluate (C) by holding fixed only the conditions *in which the mind constitutes* the world, then we will say that (C) is false. There is no one way to evaluate (C). We say either that it is true or that it is false, depending on how we evaluate it.

Does this approach yield an adequate explanation of how (C) could be both true and false? I doubt it. Certainly the same counterfactual conditional *sentence* can have different truth-values depending on which background conditions are held fixed (just as the *sentence* "Rodriguez is tall" can have different truth-values against different comparison classes). Moreover, there is clearly more flexibility in the truth-values of counterfactual conditional sentences than in those of many other sentences. But even for counterfactual conditional sentences, there are limits to how far we may vary background conditions in assigning truth-values from the actual situation.

We evaluate the counterfactual conditional sentence "If it were the case that *p*, then it would be the case that *q*," by checking whether the consequent *q* is true in the possible situation most similar to the actual situation (in all its detail) in which *p* is true. Thus, we evaluate "If Bizet and Verdi had been compatriots, Bizet would have been Italian" by judging whether Bizet is Italian in the possible situation most similar to the actual situation in which Bizet and Verdi are compatriots. In evaluating the sentence, we do not have license to consider just any possible situation in which *p* is true; we must consider the one most similar to the actual situation in all its detail. Now, we are stymied when there is no unique possible situation most similar to the actual situation in which *p* is true. In the example of Bizet and Verdi, we do not know what to say about the truth-value of the counterfactual conditional sentence. The reason is that in this case, there are two possible situations most similar to the actual one—one in which Bizet and Verdi are both French, the other in which they are both Italian—and our verdict on the truth-value of the sentence hangs on which of these situations we assume in evaluating the sentence. Without a reason to incline us to one or the other, the counterfactual conditional sentence has *no* determinate truth-value. One might protest that in this case we may choose either situation and thus assign either truth-value. In other words, the counterfactual conditional sentence has one truth-value relative to one possible situation and another relative to the other. But even if we have such latitude in our choice of situation to consider, it is clear that we do not have a perfectly free choice in which background conditions we hold fixed and which we vary. We could not, for instance, ask what would be the case if Bizet and Verdi were both Martians—unless that is required by the two of them being compatriots.

A similar point applies to (C). To be sure, if no minds had existed, things would have been much different from the way they actually are. Nevertheless, they would not have been so different that trilobites would not have existed. Consequently, we must assign true to (C): trilobites would still have existed even if no minds had existed. A situation in which an asteroid wiped out all mammals before the evolution of minds is more similar to our actual situation than a situation in which, primevally, history unfolded in such a way that trilobites never existed. Thus, we must assign true to (C). We could assign false to the sentence only by changing the meaning of (C). In short, there is no distinction between first-order and second-order vantages on which (C) is assigned opposite truth-values. The upshot is that plain realism claims victory over transcendental idealism (and transcendental realism as well).

Perhaps the transcendental idealist will retort that if the issue here is whether there is a defensible distinction between first- and second-order vantages, then it is permissible to distinguish between vantages by *specifying* which background conditions are held fixed. In other words, it is permissible to specify that the background conditions involved in the mind's constituting objects are held fixed. Given this specification, we are to consider whether, under the conditions specified, trilobites exist when minds do not exist. But since the background conditions differ in the two vantages, we end up assigning different truth-values to (C).

As plausible as this reply on behalf of the transcendental idealist may seem, it turns out on close inspection to be muddled. If the transcendental idealist wants to hold fixed the background conditions involved in the mind's constituting objects and then consider whether, under these conditions, trilobites exist when minds do not exist, I have no objection. But can this strange exercise contribute to a defense of transcendental idealism? Surely not. For this approach does not do the required job of reconciling the idealist claim that objects are constituted by minds with the commonsense claim (C). Transcendental idealism is *not* the claim that were we to consider whether, under the background conditions involved in the mind's constituting objects, trilobites (and other objects) exist when minds do not exist, we would say that trilobites do not exist. We can see that the latter claim does not amount to transcendental idealism by noting that the plain realist, who opposes transcendental idealism, can readily concede the claim. Rather, transcendental idealism is the claim that trilobites (and other objects) are constituted by the mind and hence that trilobites would not exist if minds did not exist. If what I have said about the evaluation of counterfactual conditional sentences is right, the strange exercise recently described does not make the latter counterfactual conditional sentence plausible and so does not defend transcendental idealism from doubts about that counterfactual conditional sentence, nor does it defend the distinction between first- and second-order vantages. In the end, transcendental idealism fails as a response to the counterfactual mindlessness objection. Plain realism carries the day.

VI. Semantic Ascent

I have treated the issue between realists and idealists as an ontological one, formulated in terms of objects and constitution by the mind, rather than in terms of how language is used, how it refers to objects, or what it means. In other words, I have treated the issue in what we may call first-order language, language about objects, not about language. (First-order language is not to be confused with a first-order vantage on objects.) This is how the issue between realists and idealists has traditionally been understood. In recent literature, however, the issue is more often *semantical* than ontological. It is treated by *ascent* from a first-order discussion about the constitution of objects to a second-order discussion about truth and other semantic properties of language about objects. So conceived, the issue may bear more directly on the nature of truth than I will subsequently take the ontological issue to do.

We may, however, ask whether the issue between realists and idealists ought to be treated (in part) by semantic ascent, as a dispute about truth or linguistic meaning. And we may also ask whether the semantical dispute can decide against any particular ontological positions. The most striking reason for thinking that the issue ought to be treated by semantic ascent is that the language in which the ontological issue is posed, first-order language, is itself susceptible to interpretation (indeed, it is susceptible to a charge of incoherence). This is a significant point.

It is perhaps easiest to see the force of this point about interpretation by entertaining a sample semantical view with antirealist (and antiidealist) implications: *expressivism*. The expressivist hopes to undercut any possible first-order realist victory over idealism by claiming that the apparently objectual first-order language of the ontological issue is not really what it seems. We may take ethical language as an example. One version of expressivism about ethical language is an *emotivism* according to which ethical language expresses emotions rather than attributing ethical properties to persons or actions. On emotivism, "Gandhi is a good person" means something akin to "Hurray for Gandhi" rather than "Gandhi has a certain property." The emotivist would claim to undercut any issue between moral realism and moral idealism by denying an interpretation on which moral language expresses facts that might be mind-independent or mind-dependent. Other versions of expressivism might be held to work in a similar fashion against corresponding realisms and idealisms. The proposal is that if expressivism correctly interprets first-order language, then realists cannot express their position and neither can idealists; the debate never gets off the ground.

How threatening should realists and idealists find expressivism? One reply to the expressivist challenge is that even if expressivism correctly interprets ethical or any other local branch of language, it is implausible as a *global* interpretation of language. For it depends on a contrast between objectual and nonobjectual language. And it is surely implausible to claim, as a global expressivist must, that *no* language is objectual. On the contrary, our ability to understand the contrast between these kinds of language would seem to depend on an appeal to paradigms of objectual and nonobjectual language. Emotivism about ethical language, for example, is formulated by saying that ethical language is to be assimilated to language expressing emotion like "Hurray for Gandhi" rather than to language attributing properties to objects like "This chair is a Chippendale." But then emotivism is intelligible only if some language is objectual. And the same goes for other versions of expressivism.

A rather different reply to the expressivist challenge is that if global expressivism is inconsistent with the intelligibility of the debate between realists and idealists, then we cannot assess its merits as an interpretation of language apart from considering whether the debate between realists and idealists is intelligible. We cannot simply consider the merits of global expressivism on other grounds, find in its favor, and then declare the realist-idealist debate moribund. We must consider the viability of that debate as we assess the merits of global expressivism itself. From this perspective, the apparent intelligibility of the debate poses an objection to global expressivism. Of course this is not yet to find against global expressivism or even to deny that considerations that favor global expressivism tell against realism and idealism. It is simply to observe that we cannot judge the power of global expressivism to undercut the debate apart from considerations that independently favor or undermine that debate.

We may extend this last point quite generally to any attempt to undermine realism by semantic ascent. For example, some understand the issue between realism and idealism as a dispute about whether truth is an *epistemic* matter—whether truth is a matter of the justification of belief. On a simple epistemic theory of truth,

> a proposition is true just in case believing it is justified.

In making truth a matter of justification, the epistemic theory makes it depend on the mind. For this reason it has been regarded as a version of idealism (Dummett 1978). I do not wish to deny that the dispute between epistemic and nonepistemic theories of truth may plausibly be regarded as closely analogous to the ontological issue between realism and idealism. Indeed, epistemic theories make truth depend on the mind in a way that nonepistemic theories do not. We will consider epistemic theories of truth further in Chapters 4 and 7. I do, however, wish to deny that the dispute between these theories can in isolation settle the first-order issue. One possibility is that ontological realism is left an option by the victory of an epistemic theory of truth. If, however, it is not left an option, the ontological realist can always protest that this reduces the plausibility of the epistemic theory—to zero, if the basis for rejecting the intelligibility of realism carries over to other objectual language (see Devitt and Sterelny 1989 for development of this point). For this reason, the semantical issue does not by itself settle the ontological one. This is not to deny that there could be a point to pursuing the ontological issue by semantical inquiry. It is only to say that we are not forced to do so by the allegation that some further interpretation of the issue is needed to capture the intentions of its participants.

I am inclined, then, to doubt that the realism-idealism dispute must be served by semantic ascent. There is, however, one last and converse question about semantic ascent that we must address: is the dispute between historically important theories of truth really a disguised version of that between realists and idealists? Might semantical questions, such as the nature of truth, have their interest primarily because they encode ontological questions? In my opinion, some aspects of the dispute about truth may be viewed as a disguised version of that between realists and idealists and others not. The dispute between epistemic and nonepistemic theories of truth, for example, may gain what significance it has from its analogy to or implications for the debate between realism and idealism. It may be that the issue between these theories matters largely because epistemic theories make truth depend on the mind in a way that nonepistemic theories do not. For this reason, the ontological dispute may profit from our looking into the dispute between these theories. Indeed, certain arguments for epistemic theories (e.g., the manifestation argument discussed in Chapter 4) may provide support for ontological idealism. More broadly, as I noted in the Introduction, the fundamental matter confronting the theory of truth is undoubtedly whether truth involves a relation to thinkers. This need not, however, cash out to a dispute about whether truth depends on the mind, as with epistemic vs. nonepistemic theories. It may turn on whether truth is relative to a subject (relativism vs. absolutism—see Chapter 2) or, quite differently, on whether truth involves a relation to a truth-ascriber (the correspondence theory vs. deflationism—see Chapters 5 and 6). The analogy with the realism-idealism dispute is weaker in the latter cases than it is in the case of epistemic vs. nonepistemic theories of truth.

To recap the story I have told about idealism, the view has no convincing motivation. The arguments for idealism—the epistemological and representation arguments—fail. Specific versions of idealism—r-idealism, identity idealism, phenomenalism, functional idealism, and projectivism—fall to objections specific to those versions. More important, there are two convincing general objections to idealism—the regress objection and the counterfactual mindlessness objection. And the matter of semantic ascent does not appreciably change the picture. In short, there is no defensible version of idealism. Objects do not depend for their existence on the mind.

I am inclined, therefore, to reject all the forms of idealism we have seen in this chapter: r-idealism, identity idealism, phenomenalism, functional idealism, perspectivism, and transcendental idealism. Objects are not, in any sense, even partly constituted by the mind. The existence of objects does not involve a relation to thinkers. We may embrace r-realism. We ought also to embrace plain realism.

To say this, however, is not yet to say that truth involves no relation to thinkers. On the contrary, all the historically important theories of truth agree that truth does involve *some* such relation. These theories nevertheless differ crucially in just which relation to thinkers they say truth involves. Let us, then, turn to the topic of truth and begin our investigation of what sort of relation to thinkers truth might involve.

Chapter Two

Absolutism and Relativism

The Greek Sophist Protagoras, writing in the fifth century B.C.E., was the first philosopher to formulate a view that could be interpreted as a version of relativism. A half century later, Plato undertook to refute Protagoras's relativism in Plato's dialogue the *Theaetetus* (1973b). After this lively start in ancient Greece, relativism fell out of favor and was ignored for much of the span of Western philosophy. It had few if any medieval or early modern adherents. Relativism has, however, resurfaced in our own century, and it has by this time achieved considerable popularity both within and outside of philosophy (see Hollis and Lukes 1982 for discussion of modern versions of relativism).

I. Moral Relativism

Without doubt relativism will be most familiar to modern readers as a view of *moral* truth, rather than as a fully general view of truth, and I will take advantage of this familiarity with moral relativism to limn the quite comparable merits and demerits of global relativism. We may define moral relativism this way: a proposition about the morality of an action is true for (or true relative to) a person *S* just in case the action conforms to *S*'s moral code or system of beliefs about morality. Thus, the proposition that abortion is morally permissible is true for *S* just in case, according to *S*'s moral code, abortion is morally permissible.

Moral relativism, please note, is *not* the view that whether the proposition that *S* is permitted to perform an action is true turns on whether that action conforms to *S*'s moral code. For it is not a view restricted to pronouncing on the truth-values of propositions about the morality of *S*'s actions. Rather, it pertains to *all* moral propositions and hence all actions that fall under morality, whether those of *S* or others.

Thus, moral relativism differs significantly from moral subjectivism, on which a proposition about the morality of a subject *S*'s action (e.g., "Abortion is morally permissible for *S*") is true just in case that action conforms to *S*'s moral code. Moral subjectivism is in fact a version of moral absolutism, in effect assigning morally permissible actions to subjects on the basis of their codes. Moral relativism, by contrast, does not assign morally permissible actions to subjects at all. On the contrary, it denies that there is a unique assignment of morally permissible actions to subjects.

We might regard moral subjectivism as an *antiuniversalist* thesis about moral truth: it denies that there are moral principles that bind the actions of all subjects. Moral relativism, on the other hand, does not deny universalism about moral truth. On the contrary, it seeks a way to make room for a certain universality about moral principles under a certain democracy about moral truth. The democracy about moral truth consists of the view that conflicting moral propositions are true for different subjects. Under this kind of democracy, which moral relativism honors by relativizing moral truth to a subject, moral relativism can admit the universality of moral principles, relative to at least some subjects. The universalism about moral principles consists of the universal bindingness of moral principles (relative to a subject). Relative to a subject, moral principles are universally binding when, according to the subject's moral code, these principles bind the actions of all morally similar agents. It is indeed one point of relativism to make room for such a universalism under a democratic view of moral truth. Thus, moral relativism is consistent with something denied by moral subjectivism. In spirit, moral relativism aims ninety degrees away from moral subjectivism. Moral subjectivism aims to deny a certain universalism about moral principles, while moral relativism aims to make room for a universalism about moral principles.

The idea of making room for such universalism under a democracy about moral truth is attractive. One reason this approach is attractive is that it is hard to see how to escape this universalism. Universalism about moral principles undergirds our most common and intuitive thinking about the application of moral principles. To argue, for example, that the civil rights possessed by heterosexuals should extend to gay people as well is to assume that the same moral principles bind two groups of people when there is no morally relevant difference between these people—in other words, that moral principles are universal. It is very hard to see how to reconcile moral subjectivism with such reasoning. To effect a reconciliation of moral subjectivism with such universalist reasoning about moral principles, it would be necessary to suppose that it is always a decisive morally relevant difference between individuals that they hold different moral codes. Once we make this supposition, the moral subjectivist can say that the same moral principles are binding on two groups of people when there is no morally relevant difference between these people. But the supposition itself is preposterous. There are too many other human psychological and social features that seem morally relevant to suppose that morally relevant differences always turn decisively on the moral codes individuals hold.

To take an example, some Indian women allegedly prefer that their capacity for skills or their innate talents of various kinds not be developed. Whether or not this is so, it is at least conceivable that there be a society something like the one they allegedly live in, in which a shared moral code discourages or even prohibits these women from developing these capacities. Yet, I take it, we do not think that whether it is true that they ought to develop these capacities rests exclusively on their possessing this moral code. If there is anything to be said against their developing their capacities, it must stem in part from the nature of their society and the role they play in it. Note that the thought that whatever is to be said against their developing their capacities must stem from the nature of their society is not merely consistent with universalism about moral principles but driven by it. But this same thought is inconsistent with moral subjectivism. As long as individuals live in a society with a certain nature and play a certain role in it, they will be governed by certain moral principles, regardless of their moral codes. Of course the moral subjectivist might respond to this line of criticism by denying that a society can have a morally relevant nature or that individuals can play a morally relevant role unless these individuals possess a moral code that subscribes to the principle. In my view, it is doubtful that the moral subjectivist can make a case for this response. But in any event such a response would concede that moral codes always vary with features that are intuitively morally relevant. And this concession would make moral subjectivism extensionally equivalent to a universalist view that does not mention moral codes. The concession would, in other words, pull the subjectivist punch from moral subjectivism.

It does not seem, then, that moral subjectivism can be squared with universalism about moral principles while maintaining its independence from apparently quite different universalist views about moral principles. Moral relativism, in contrast, can be squared with universalism about moral principles without any loss of integrity. Indeed, it is a major point of moral relativism to leave room for universalism about moral principles, as long as that universalism is itself relativized to a subject. That is, moral relativism seeks to leave room for the universally binding character of moral principles. But it does so in a way that makes such universality relative to a subject. It is in this way that moral relativism makes room for universalism about moral principles under democracy about moral truth. To be sure, moral relativism does not by itself *guarantee* universalism about moral principles relative to all subjects. Whether moral principles are universal relative to a subject depends on that subject's moral code—in particular, on whether the principles in that code are universally binding. But moral relativism can at least allow universality in a way that moral subjectivism cannot. I am inclined to think that, in this regard, moral relativism's advantage over moral subjectivism is decisive. Any plausible view of moral principles must admit moral universalism in some way.

What of the moral relativist's development of democracy about moral truth? I am inclined to think that the case for such democracy is less impressive than the case for moral universalism. A view capable of expressing democracy about moral truth may seem attractive because there may seem no reason to favor one person's moral code over another's. Disagreement about moral principles is reputedly widespread and intractable. But there is no neutral basis for resolving the disagreement. Consequently, there is no reason to prefer the code of one person or culture to that of another. Moral relativism has the advantage of absolving us of the need to admit that one person's code is preferable to that of another.

There are, however, various problems with this brief for moral democracy. One is its pat assumption that there are widespread and intractable disagreements about moral principles. In judging whether disagreements about what people ought to do are really disagreements about moral principles or codes, one must take care to rule out the possibility that the disagreement is not really a disagreement about moral principles at all but rather turns on a nonmoral matter—e.g, on morally relevant nonmoral facts (such as whether there is an afterlife, whether one will be punished in the afterlife for one's moral transgressions, or whether fetuses are persons). People who disagree, for example, about whether abortion is morally permissible may agree on all the relevant moral principles and disagree only on whether these principles apply to a fetus because they disagree on whether the fetus is a person. The latter disagreement concerns morally relevant nonmoral facts; it is not a disagreement about moral principles. In judging apparently moral disagreements, one must also take care to rule out the possibility that these disagreements are not really disagreements at all but derive from differences in the morally relevant nonmoral conditions in which people live (e.g., differences in the degree of scarcity of food, shelter, and other resources). People who apparently disagree over whether theft should receive harsh punishment may agree on all the relevant moral principles and merely appear to disagree about the appropriate punishment for theft because they have different societal conditions in mind. Under conditions of scarcity, theft may be a much more serious offense than under conditions of abundance, and may accordingly merit much harsher punishment. In short, it is no easy matter to be sure that apparent disagreements about moral principles really concern those principles or, for that matter, constitute disagreements at all.

Even setting aside these problems with the argument for democracy, we may question the argument's assumption that intractable disagreement should incline us to democracy. There is intractable disagreement about the afterlife and the nature of God, but few are tempted by this to infer that there are no facts of these matters or that the truth about them is merely relative. Few are willing to infer from disagreement about theology or the afterlife that there is no fact of the matter as to whether God exists or whether the soul is immortal. Virtually every party to these disputes will maintain, even in the face of intractable disagreement, that one side is right. This shows at least that intractable disagreement by itself has little intuitive force in favor of relativism, at least of kinds other than moral. Even if we find some feature of the moral case that in combination with intractable disagreement, does favor moral relativism, that feature is evidently missing from the examples of the afterlife and God. So this feature is not a *global* feature of discourse, and the argument from disagreement cannot yield the result that *all* truth-values are relative. There are other difficulties with the argument from disagreement, but the points we have so far made will perhaps suffice to discourage employing the argument to establish global relativism.

II. Relativism

I have taken moral relativism as an example of relativism both because it is familiar and because it is an attractive version of relativism. Relativism about other matters—physics or psychology, say—has considerably less intuitive pull. These versions of relativism would presumably arise from parallel arguments from disagreement. But for nonmoral propositions, as I have already noted, we have far less temptation to infer relativism from widespread and intractable disagreement. Thus, the argument from disagreement is unlikely to establish a global relativism, one on which all truth-values are relative. At the same time, the argument from disagreement is the most likely source of any nonmoral relativism. For this reason, it seems best to take relativism to be the weaker view that there are relative truth-values, rather than the stronger, global view that all truth-values are relative. I will call the weaker view "unrestricted" relativism or just "relativism" for short. Thus we may define unrestricted absolutism and relativism in this way:

> *Absolutism*: All truth-values are truth-values simpliciter.
>
> *Relativism*: At least some truth-values are relative truth-values—truth-values relative to a person, culture, system of beliefs, cognitive framework, intellectual perspective, or conceptual scheme.

These definitions may seem to swing from one extreme to another—from making relativism too strong to making absolutism too strong. But I believe that absolutism is defensible even in this strong formulation. Note that relativism, as I understand it, does not relativize truth to a truth-*ascriber*—to one who ascribes truth to a proposition. Rather, a truth-ascriber relativizes truth to a *subject* or *system of beliefs*.

Relativism about truth is not to be confused with the *linguistic* relativism of Benjamin Whorf (1956) and Edward Sapir (1949), according to which languages reflect, express, or embody radically different ontological theories. Linguistic relativism is an *empirical* claim, while relativism about truth is an a priori semantical theory. Relativism about truth is quite consistent with the denial of linguistic relativism, and vice versa. And absolutism about truth is likewise consistent with linguistic relativism. (See Devitt and Sterelny 1989 for a critical discussion of linguistic relativism.)

Perhaps this is an opportune moment to remark on the bearing of the dispute between absolutism and relativism on various other disputes with which we are concerned in this book—notably, the dispute between realism and idealism and the debate among theories of truth. It is natural to assimilate the issue between absolutism and relativism to the dispute between realism and idealism. This assimilation is warranted up to a point. It is natural for realists to accept absolutism. Idealists, however, need not accept relativism. But it is worth noting that one version of idealism plausibly leads to relativism. I have in mind *perspectivism* (Nietzsche 1979). According to perspectivism, there is no single world. Rather, there are various perspectives from which things are viewed, and there is a world-from-perspective *P* for each perspective *P*. If truth is then understood as correspondence to the world-from-a-perspective, relativism follows. Thus, a certain version of idealism arguably leads to relativism.

In this connection, it is worth noting too that the arguments for absolutism and relativism and the objections to the views are quite analogous to those regarding realism and idealism. Indeed, relativism may be defensible, as idealism is, only on the assumption of transcendental idealism. And relativism may therefore suffer a major drawback of idealism: the fact that transcendental idealism is implausible. I will say more about this in the next section. In the meantime, we may observe that, from a logical point of view, there is nothing to prevent one from combining absolutism and idealism (assuming that one can consistently accept arguments for and rebut objections to the views in these combinations).

Just as the issue between absolutism and relativism is often assimilated to the dispute between realism and idealism, it is also often assimilated to the dispute between correspondence theories of truth and coherence theories of truth. This assimilation, too, is warranted up to a point. Though classical versions of pragmatism and coherentism have been absolutist, these views may be defensible only on the assumption of relativism. We ought not, however, to carry the assimilation of these disputes too far. The correspondence theory, as I have already suggested, may be tendered in either an absolutist or a relativist version.

III. Objections to Relativism

We now have enough grasp of relativism to be able to review the standard objections to the view. I find some of these objections persuasive.

The Platonic Objection

In the *Theaetetus* (1973b), Plato famously rejected the relativism of Protagoras, offering the following objection (but see Burnyeat 1976 for a contrary interpretation of Plato). Consider the statement of relativism itself, that some truths are relative to a subject or system of beliefs. For ease of reference call the statement of relativism *R*. The relativist of course claims *R*. But for any <*p*>, <*p*> entails that <*p*> is true. (I will write "<*p*>" for "the proposition that *p*.") Hence, *R* entails that *R* is true. Consequently, the relativist is committed, not only to *R*, but to the claim that *R* is true. Now, the objection continues, *R* might be claimed true in either of two senses. It might be claimed *absolutely* true, or it might be claimed only *relatively* true. But *R* cannot be claimed *absolutely* true, if the relativist is to be consistent. For relativism is inconsistent with *R*'s being an absolute truth. This is obviously so on a version of relativism that holds that *all* truths are relative. But it is also plausible on the unrestricted relativism with which we are dealing, according to which *some* truths are relative. To be sure, as we have defined unrestricted relativism, it does not entail that *every* truth is relative. But presumably propositions about which there is entrenched disagreement would be relatively true or false if any propositions are. And since *R* is a proposition about which there is entrenched disagreement, the relativist is committed by *R* itself to the view that *R* is merely relatively, not absolutely true. So *R* cannot be claimed absolutely true. The only alternative, of course, is that *R* is relatively true. But then the relativist must admit that *R* may be true relative to some systems and not others. And this, according to the objection, is an untenable position for the relativist.

Now, the objector must concede that the conclusion that *R* may be true relative to some systems and not others is not strictly speaking inconsistent with relativism. On the contrary, the relativist only claims *R*, and presumably, that claim entails, for the relativist, only that *R* is true relative to the *relativist*'s system. It is quite consistent with this that *R* be false relative to other systems (e.g., relative to an absolutist's system). Nevertheless, the objection maintains, the conclusion that *R* may be false relative to other systems tells against relativism. To be sure, relative to the relativist's system, relativism is true. But at the same time, relative to an absolutist's system, relativism may well be false. Nor can the relativist claim any sort of victory here on the ground that relativism is after all true relative to the relativist's system. Such a victory would be Pyrrhic. For the absolutist may equally claim victory. This clash of victories suggests that no one has won and indeed raises a doubt about whether there could have been a genuine dispute to begin with. If the relativist is forced to admit all this, then, the objection goes, that is surely a significant flaw in relativism. The absolutist, by contrast, is not forced to admit that relativism may be true in any comparable way.

Is this Platonic objection to relativism convincing? It is tough to size up the points about victory, but the objection fails even waiving the plausibility of these points. For the relativist may reply by refusing to concede that absolutism is true relative to an absolutist system. What is true relative to a system is (assuming for the sake of discussion an epistemic version of relativism) whatever is ideally warranted in that system. (On a pragmatic version of relativism, by contrast, what is true is whatever it is useful to believe.) The relativist of course holds that *relativism* is ideally warranted relative to any system—even an absolutist system. So the relativist need not concede that the victory of relativism is Pyrrhic or that there is no genuine issue between relativism and absolutism. Of course if one believes that the upshot of the issue between relativism and absolutism is that relativism is mistaken, one will deny that relativism is ideally warranted in every system. But this merely shows that the Platonic objection gives way to other arguments for and against relativism. If those other arguments favor relativism, then the relativist can meet the Platonic objection. If, on the other hand, those arguments do not favor relativism, then the Platonic objection is unnecessary to defeat relativism. In either case, the Platonic objection is a dispensable fifth wheel in the debate between relativism and absolutism.

The Meaning Objection

A second standard objection to relativism appeals to a widely shared and perhaps unavoidable principle of linguistic meaning (Newton-Smith 1982). The relevant principle of meaning is

> (M) Sameness of meaning entails sameness of truth-value: if sentences *S* and *T* mean the same thing, then *S* and *T* have the same truth-value.[1]

For example, according to (M), the sentence "Some bachelors are tall" has the same truth-value as the sentence "Some unmarried men are tall," since the two sentences mean the same thing. It is indeed hard to see how they could diverge in truth-value, given that "bachelor" means the same as "unmarried man," and the sentences both predicate "tall" of some bachelor or unmarried man.

Principle (M) is in fact common ground among the theories of meaning that have been most influential in this century. The principle is indeed secured by any theory of meaning on which the meaning of a sentence is defined as something that determines the truth-value of the sentence (given certain other background conditions, such as those that obtain in uttering the sentence with the meaning it has). We may call such theories of meaning *truth-theoretic* theories of meaning (for the purest example, see Davidson 1984b, 1984c). Principle (M) is entailed not only by truth-theoretic theories of meaning but by other theories of meaning as well. For example, it is entailed by a theory of meaning that makes the meaning of a sentence identical with the standard communicative intention with which the sentence is used—a theory usually called *Gricean* after its proponent, the philosopher of language Paul Grice (see Schiffer 1972 for a full development of the idea).

Now how does principle (M) bear on relativism? Simply put, (M) contradicts relativism. For on relativism there are sentences that mean the same in their use relative to two systems even though relative to one system they are true and relative to the other system they are not true. Indeed, it is the whole point of relativism to maintain that sentences with the same meaning can have different truth-values relative to different systems. It follows that relativism is inconsistent with (M) and thus inconsistent with a credible theory of meaning.

How forceful is this "meaning" objection to relativism? Quite forceful. Clearly the relativist must shun any theory of meaning on which sameness of meaning entails sameness of truth-value. Yet it is doubtful that there are any viable theories of meaning left for the relativist after we have purged the ones that obey principle (M).

The problem, in a nutshell, is that the alternatives to a truth-theoretic theory of meaning, at least the ones that have so far been proposed, are highly sensitive to differences of context. By "context," I mean the nonlinguistic surroundings in which language is used, including psychological attitudes, social relations, and nonverbal behavior. The relativist has difficulty turning from a truth-theoretic theory of meaning to a nontruth-theoretic theory because theories of the latter sort tend to be more sensitive to context than truth-theoretic theories of meaning. In fact, one point in favor of truth-theoretic theories of meaning was always that these theories avoided oversensitivity to context. Truth-theoretic theories render meaning invariant across contexts precisely by tying meaning rigidly to truth-values. But these theories are able to make meaning invariant across contexts only by staking the invariance of meaning on stable truth-values. This requires truth-values that are constant across contexts. Without stable truth-values, it is unclear whether there is any way to keep meaning invariant across contexts. It is no surprise that non-truth-theoretic theories of meaning that forgo tying meaning to truth-values entail variations in meaning across contexts, hence across situations of the kind in which relativists would claim that each of a pair of contradictory statements is relatively true. Yet if meaning varies across these situations, then the relativist cannot claim that there are contradictory statements across systems.

A thorough discussion of the impediments to combining non-truth-theoretic theories of meaning with relativism would take us into the thickets of the theory of meaning, far afield from our concerns about truth, and we don't have time for that. Let me instead illustrate the impediments to this combination of theories with one non-truth-theoretic theory of meaning, a *use* theory.

On a use theory of meaning, the meaning of a sentence is identified with its use—which is presumably the sum of its linguistic and nonlinguistic uses. A use theory subscribes to the principle:

> If two sentences have the same meaning, then they have the same use.

Might the relativist adopt a use theory of meaning? On the positive side it appears that a use theory may contradict principle (M). For it may be that the use of a sentence can be defined in such a way that sameness of use does not entail sameness of truth-value. And if this is so, then on a use theory of meaning, sameness of meaning does not entail sameness of truth-value. So a use theory may, by rejecting (M), avert the meaning objection to relativism.

But on the negative side, it is not at all clear that the relativist can adopt a use theory of meaning. For a use theory may preclude sameness of meaning under disagreement. That is, a use theory may preclude one culture from employing a sentence with the same meaning as another culture if those two cultures disagree. For the use of a sentence may vary depending on how much the language users disagree. And if the use of a sentence varies enough across cultures, then the sentence does *not* count as having the same use in the two cultures. Thus, on the use theory it does not count as having the same meaning. But of course the relativist needs to be able to cite examples (at least possible ones) of disagreement across cultures. For relativism has a point only if there are cases of such disagreement. Thus, it is unclear whether the relativist can adopt a use theory of meaning. Perhaps the relativist can loosen up the notion of the use of sentences in such a way as to allow the sameness of the use of sentences under disagreement across cultures, as long as the disagreement is not extensive. This would, however, prevent the relativist from assigning relative truth-values across cultures that extensively disagree. Unfortunately, the current state of the use theory of meaning rules out any definitive judgment as to whether relativism is consistent with the use theory. The use theory is, at this point, simply too underdeveloped to supply the kind of criterion of individuation of uses of sentences that would make it possible to judge firmly whether a sentence is or is not used in the same way in two cultures. But on the face of it, a use theory of meaning is less suited to relativism than are certain alternatives to it (alternatives which we will consider in the next section).

It isn't clear at this point whether the relativist has any option for a theory of meaning. And without a theory of meaning, we can't ascertain whether the relativist is right in claiming that there are instances where people disagree without genuinely disagreeing—instances, in other words, in which truth is relative. The upshot of all this is that the meaning objection poses a serious threat to relativism.

The Regress Objection

In my opinion, the most crippling objection to relativism is that it generates a vicious regress analogous to the regress generated by idealism (discussed in Chapter 1). The regress arises in this way. The relativist must explain relative truth by cashing it out in nonrelative terms, as for example in "belief" relativism:

> <*p*> is true relative to person or system *S* just in case *S* believes *p*.

For we speak a language that is, on the face of it, unrelativized, and we don't understand talk of relative truth until such talk is explicated in a language we understand—in other words, in unrelativized language. But once the relativist offers such an explication, he or she faces the following dilemma.

Either the truth-value of the right-hand side—*S* believes *p*—is to be understood as *implicitly* relativized to some particular person (or system of beliefs) *S*, or it isn't. Suppose the relativist embraces the second horn of the dilemma: the right-hand side is *not* understood as implicitly relativized to some *S*. Then the right-hand side has a unique truth-value, and we cannot avoid the question what makes it have a particular truth-value—e.g., true. Presumably, in this case, there is no alternative to saying that what makes the right-hand side true is (at least in part) that *S* believes *p*. Whatever else may be involved in its being true, part of what makes <*S* believes *p*> true is that *S* believes *p*. This by itself presents the relativist with no problem, since relativism entails only that some truths are relative, and thus relativism may exempt the proposition that *S* believes *p* from being a relative truth. Trouble arises, however, when we reflect that for the latter proposition to be absolutely true in the way envisioned, there must be a person or system *S* and a belief *p*. And if there is a person *S* and a belief *p*, then presumably whatever must be the case for there to be such things must exist too—e.g., a brain, oxygen, and so on. In other words, there has to be (a certain fragment of?) the world. But if this much of the world exists, then it is very difficult for the relativist to avoid admitting that for given propositions <*p*>, what makes <*p*> true is (at least in part) that *p*. That is, it is not merely that what makes <*S* believes *p*> true is that *S* believes *p*; it is also that what makes <*p*> true is that *p*. But in this case, *no* propositions are relatively true. The upshot of all this is that if the right-hand side of the formula is not understood as implicitly relativized to some *S*, then truths are absolute, and there is no point in talking of relative truth. Absolutism holds and relativism is mistaken.

It seems, then, that the relativist must recoil from the second horn of the dilemma to embrace its first horn. The relativist must understand the right-hand side of the relativist explication of relative truth—that *S* believes *p*—as *implicitly* relativized to the system of some person *T*. That is, the right-hand side must be assumed to have a truth-value implicitly relativized to some system—the system of *T*. But if the right-hand side is implicitly relativized to the system of some *T*, then the relativist explication of relative truth has not yet specified a truth-value for <*p*>. For the explication asks us, in effect, to consider <*S* believes *p*> as true relative to *T*. But it is precisely the task of the explication to secure truth-values for such attributions of relative truth. Since the relativist has not yet completed the task of securing truth-values for attributions of relative truth, the explication does not yet give us a truth-value. The relativist could of course treat "<*S* believes *p*> is true relative to *T*" as itself implicitly relativized to a *further* person or system *U*. But in this event, we are off to the races. The point of the explication was precisely to fix the truth-value of <*p*> relative to the system of *S*. In other words, the dilemma forces relativism to renounce any fixed truth-values at all, even relative ones. Yet it is precisely the business of a theory of truth (in conjunction with surrounding conditions) to fix such values. Thus, the first horn of the dilemma is no more hospitable to the relativist than is the second horn.

To summarize the dilemma, if the right-hand side is taken as explicitly relativized, then truth-values are absolute, contradicting relativism. But if it is taken as implicitly relativized, then relativism fails in a prime task of a theory of truth—fixing truth-values. Either way, relativism is untenable and must be rejected. In my opinion, this regress objection mounts a decisive case against relativism.

By now it should be manifest that I regard the meaning objection to relativism as formidable and the regress objection as insurmountable. The regress objection in particular undermines the viability, and even the coherence, of relativism. The objection shows that no proposition has a relative truth-value. It establishes absolutism, assuming that truth-values must be either relative or absolute. The case for absolutism over relativism will matter in the chapters that follow because pragmatism and coherentism about truth are arguably committed to denying absolutism. The failure of relativism undermines these historically important theories of truth as well.

IV. Neither an Absolutist nor a Relativist Be?

Before we close our discussion of absolutism and relativism, it is worth considering briefly whether there is any room for an intermediate position between the two views. Here I do not have in mind the view that some truth-values are absolute and others relative; this view is ruled out by the meaning and regress objections to relativism. Rather, I have in mind the alternative views that many, or perhaps all, statements have truth-values that are neither relative nor absolute, and that many (or all) statements lack truth-values altogether. I am inclined to believe that there is room for an intermediate position here. At the same time, I doubt whether there is any motivation for accepting such a position. At least, I can see no motivation for doing so in any of the ideas to which one would naturally look for middle ground between absolutism and relativism.

There are several ideas to which one would naturally look for middle ground. There is, for example, the idea, associated with the contemporary philosopher of science Thomas Kuhn (1962), that there are, on certain topics, alternative, incommensurable descriptions of the world (i.e., apparently inconsistent descriptions whose meanings differ in ways that deprive them of genuine inconsistency). I will, however, take my cue from another source, the later work of the twentieth-century Austrian philosopher Ludwig Wittgenstein (1958).

One idea suggested by the work of Wittgenstein is that there are different linguistic practices or "language games" for different forms of life—religious, mathematical, moral, psychological, and so on. The rules of these language games determine which statements are appropriately made in the course of the activities of those forms of life, in something like the way the rules of chess determine which moves are appropriately made in a game of chess. Now, here is the point that might be thought relevant to the plausibility of an alternative to relativism. These games are related to one another and to what exists in a manner that makes it misleading to say that statements made under the rules of the games describe a single world. For the meanings of statements are determined by their role, or in other words by their use, in human life. The use of a statement is a matter of what speakers do with it. Statements do not derive their meaning from describing the world but from their linguistic and nonlinguistic uses. The idea here bears some resemblance to the functional idealism characterized in Chapter 1, the view that objects have their features and exist in virtue of their role in human life. The difference between the present view and functional idealism, however, is that the present view concerns the meaning of statements rather than the existence of objects.

It might be thought that this use theory of meaning rules out absolutism and relativism. First, the theory might be thought to rule out absolutism. For statements are endowed with meaning by their linguistic and nonlinguistic use; they do not mean what they do because they describe the world. From this it might be thought to follow that saying that a statement is *true* does not describe the world but rather equips us for getting along in the world. If this is so, statements are not made true by facts in the world, and they are not constrained by the facts to have a unique truth-value. Consequently, it might be claimed, statements do not have absolute truth-values.

At the same time, it might be thought that the use theory of meaning entails that relativism is mistaken. For language games are distinguished by the use of language; the conditions of use differ in different language games. But then, on a use theory of meaning, the statements employed in different language games do not share their meanings. And so they are not inconsistent with each other. Since relativism demands inconsistent systems of belief, relativism does not apply. In short, the use theory and the language game approach might be thought to offer an alternative to both absolutism and relativism.

Note that even if this is so, the language game approach does not deny that there is a unique world or that statements can be true or false. Rather, it refuses a certain way of thinking of these claims. It refuses to treat statements as deriving their meaning or truth-conditions from describing something, the world, to which the statements are related. (See McDowell 1984 for a parallel Wittgensteinian rejection of the debate between realists and idealists, this time based on Wittgenstein's views about rule-following.)

I am inclined to concede that the language game approach, assuming it can be made coherent and plausible, has some chance of excluding relativism. The use theory of meaning may well entail that statements employed in different language games do not share their meaning—a point inconsistent with relativism. Whether it does entail this depends on the answers to some very hard questions about the relation between the use of language and its meaning—on just which uses determine meaning and on the exact way in which uses of language are individuated within and across cultures. The issues here are the same as those we discussed under the meaning objection to relativism. The language game approach may well prevail against relativism.

But even if the approach does prevail against relativism, I cannot see that it also makes any headway against absolutism. For a use theory of meaning does not by itself entail that saying a statement is true does not describe the world. Nor does it entail that statements are not made true by facts. First, the use theory is quite consistent with the claim that one use of a statement recognized by its meaning is to describe the world. Second, there is slack between the use theory of meaning and the theory of truth. In particular, a use theory is consistent with a theory of truth that fastens on one specific aspect of the use of language—e.g., description—as the use relevant to truth. In this case, the use theory may allow that statements are made true by facts. Absolutism may hold. The Wittgensteinian view does not by itself defeat absolutism. This is not to say that the view could not be developed in such a way as to be inconsistent with absolutism. But where is the argument that it must be inconsistent with absolutism—that describing the world must be excluded from the semantically relevant uses of language? As far as I can ascertain, the standard case for such an exclusion is that it enables the proponent of a use theory to deny absolutism. But of course, appeal to this reason for exclusion would beg the question against absolutism. The case against absolutism must then fall back on whatever other objections to absolutism might seem persuasive. In the absence of an independent reason to deny absolutism, there seems no motivation to pursue an intermediate position on which many or all statements have truth-values that are neither absolute nor relative or on which many or all statements lack truth-values. An intermediate position may be possible. But I see no motivation for accepting such a position—at least, no motivation in the ideas to which one would naturally look to develop middle ground between absolutism and relativism.

In this chapter we have scouted arguments for and against relativism and absolutism, and we have considered whether there is a case for an intermediate position between the views. The language game approach to language does not by itself secure an intermediate position. The epistemological argument for relativism is frail, and there are imposing objections to the view. The meaning objection to relativism has force, and the regress objection is decisive. Our conclusion is that truth cannot be relativized to a system of beliefs. This is one key respect in which truth does *not* involve a relation to thinkers. To say this is of course not to deny that truth can in *some* respect involve a relation to thinkers—e.g., by involving a relation to the *ascriber* of truth, as on deflationism. In subsequent chapters, we will explore further respects in which truth might involve a relation to thinkers.

Chapter Three

Pragmatism

With the preceding ruminations on absolutism, relativism, realism, and idealism behind us, we may embark on our study of the historically important theories of truth—the correspondence theory, pragmatism, coherentism, and deflationism. I will begin, out of historical order, with the pragmatic theory of truth.

Pragmatism is an invention of nineteenth-century American philosophy—an approach to philosophy pioneered by Charles Sanders Peirce (1931-1958) and William James (1907, 1909), and subsequently developed by John Dewey (1938). These philosophers shared a conception of philosophy as making sense of any concept by tying it to human practice and experience. In line with this conception, Peirce proposed a pragmatic theory of meaning, which was adopted in some form by both James and Dewey. James, for his part, advertised in addition a pragmatic theory of truth. I will focus in this chapter on the Jamesian pragmatic theory of truth. I will, however, say a word at the end of the chapter about the pragmatic theory of meaning and its bearing on the theory of truth that shares its name.

I. The Pragmatic Theory of Truth

James had diverse things to say about truth, and I would be hard put to weld them into a single coherent theory of truth. James himself cared little for consistency, and there would surely be something comical in laboring on his behalf in a project for which he would have had nothing but contempt. I will instead take my cue, selectively, from such remarks as these:

> The possession of true thoughts means everywhere the possession of invaluable instruments of action. (1907, 97)

> The true is only the expedient in our way of thinking, just as the right is only the expedient in our way of behaving. (1909, vii)

From these and many similar pronouncements, we may extract a simple pragmatic theory of truth:

$<p>$ is true just in case it is useful to believe that p.

Calling such a theory of truth "pragmatic" is apt. For it defines truth in terms of utility—in particular, the utility of belief. Moreover, the theory makes the concept of truth itself useful; for it is useful to think about what it is useful to believe.

The pragmatic theory clearly makes truth a relation to believers, since it makes it a matter of what it is useful to believe, and what it is useful to believe is what it is useful for *believers* to believe. Whether the theory goes so far as to make truth depend on the mind in any fashion analogous to idealism (as epistemic theories of truth do) is hard to say. It is certainly not a version of r-idealism: it does not entail that truth is (in part) created by anyone's representations. But the theory might still be viewed as claiming that truth is in some sense constituted in part by the mind, because truth is determined by what it is useful to believe, and this is determined in part by the mind.

Pragmatism could be, and perhaps in the end must be, formulated relativistically, since whether it is useful to believe a proposition evidently varies from one believer to another; so, on pragmatism, truth must vary from one believer to another. It is possible, however, that pragmatism can stave off relativism by a trick: index truth to the truth-ascriber. On such an indexical version of pragmatism, a proposition would be true when belief in the proposition is useful for the truth-ascriber. So formulated, pragmatism would join the issue between the correspondence theory and deflationism that we will address in Chapters 5 and 6: whether truth involves a relation to a truth-ascriber.

These are remarks on the general tenor of pragmatism about truth. Before we proceed to an evaluation of the view, however, two more aspects of the view will need clarification. One concerns the *kind* of usefulness necessary for truth. There are perhaps two kinds of usefulness that might be relevant to pragmatism (Lovejoy 1908, Russell 1967). One is *behavioral* usefulness. A belief is behaviorally useful when it empowers us to satisfy our desires. Such empowerment may encompass any number of abilities—to manipulate or acquire objects, to predict the future, to convince others to do things, or to communicate information to others. A belief is *cognitively* useful when it equips us to organize, predict, and explain our experience. Let it be noted that a pragmatist who emphasizes cognitive usefulness to the exclusion of behavioral usefulness will end up with a view of truth much like the coherence theory of truth. Since we will deal with that theory in the next chapter, we may assume here, as James in any event apparently does, that usefulness is some combination of behavioral and cognitive usefulness.

A second aspect of pragmatism that needs clarification is the *degree* of utility required for truth. The theory tacitly assumes that usefulness can be measured in some way. For it assumes that beliefs can be assigned a degree of usefulness on a scale of natural numbers or perhaps integers (including negative numbers, to represent harmfulness). The pragmatic account of truth might set an *absolute* lower bound on the degree of usefulness required for truth. Alternatively, it might make usefulness a *comparative* matter. If the theory sets an absolute lower bound on the degree of usefulness, then it will say that

> <*p*> is true just in case believing *p* is useful to at least degree *l*,

where *l* is the lower bound on the degree of usefulness required for truth. The trouble with such an absolute account is that there is nothing to prevent it from being the case that, for some <*p*>, believing *p* and believing not-*p* are each useful to at least degree *l*. But then, on the absolute account, these contradictory beliefs would both be true. And this is an absurd result. The comparative version of pragmatism may avoid this difficulty. The comparative account would say that <*p*> is true just in case believing *p* is more useful than certain competing actions (or inactions), such as believing not-*p*. One such comparative account would be this:

> <*p*> is true just in case believing *p* is more useful than believing not-*p*.

This account avoids the difficulty facing the absolute account, since it does not allow contradictions to be true. It does, however, face another difficulty: there may well be situations in which believing *p* and believing not-*p* are equally useful. In this case, the account will entail, implausibly, that neither *p* nor not-*p* is true. In other words, the comparative account fails to guarantee the completeness of truth. While there are no doubt indeterminacies of truth-value (as in borderline vagueness—a matter we will take up in Chapter 5), the comparative account may well entail, incorrectly, that there are indeterminacies of truth-value (neither true nor false) in cases in which, intuitively, the propositions are either true or false. I will say more on this point when we consider objections to pragmatism. For now, we may observe that whatever the difficulties with the comparative account, it is preferable to the absolute account in ruling out contradictory truths.

II. Arguments for the Pragmatic Theory of Truth

Two arguments favor pragmatism about truth:

The Pragmatic Argument

Pragmatism has the virtue of recovering and explaining a platitude about truth: the truth matters. It is a commonplace that believing the truth is useful. Much human cognition is directed toward forming true beliefs and avoiding false beliefs, and one reason people so vigorously pursue true beliefs is that they recognize the usefulness of believing the truth. Pragmatism explains why it is useful to believe what is true: believing the truth just is, by definition, believing what it is useful to believe. Pragmatism may also explain at the same time why it is commonplace to think that it is useful to believe what is true: people recognize that believing the truth is useful because the very concept of truth entails that this is so. In any event, the fact that pragmatism explains the platitude about truth may be taken to favor pragmatism.

Whether this pragmatic argument for pragmatism has force, however, very much depends on whether there is an equally attractive competing explanation of the usefulness of true beliefs, an explanation that does *not* assume that true beliefs are *by definition* useful. Here is one competing explanation: it is useful to believe truths because, as a matter of the contingent constitution of human beings and their relation to their environment, believing truths enables one to engage in useful or desire-satisfying action—action in which one would not engage if one failed to believe the truth. On this competing explanation, believing the truth that, say, wolves are dangerous enables and causes us to avoid wolves, and if we did not believe this, we would not avoid wolves. Of course believing some falsehood about wolves *might* equally impel one to avoid wolves. For example, believing the falsehood that wolves are vicious might impel one to do so. But in general, if believing this falsehood does impel one to avoid wolves, this is because one *infers* from one's false belief that wolves are vicious some *truth* that causes one to avoid wolves—e.g., the truth that wolves are dangerous. Thus, we can account for the utility of true beliefs without adverting to the pragmatic definition of truth. Moreover, this is an obvious explanation, available to just about anyone, and so, like the pragmatic definition, it promises an account, not only of the utility of true belief, but also of why it is commonplace to regard believing the truth as useful.

We now have before us an explanation of the usefulness of true beliefs that competes with the pragmatic explanation. It contrasts with the latter in several respects. For one thing, unlike the pragmatic explanation, it allows true beliefs to be useless. On the pragmatic theory, *all* true beliefs are useful, by the definition of "true." This difference will turn out in due course to favor the competing explanation. For another thing, the competing explanation allows useful false beliefs. Pragmatism, at least in the version we have so far considered, excludes useful false beliefs. This difference, too, will favor the competing explanation. Perhaps the most important difference, however, is that the competing explanation is *contingent*: true beliefs are useful because we are contingently constituted and situated in our environment in such a way that we can usually satisfy our desires only by relying in some way on true beliefs. This is a contingent explanation in the sense that it allows that useful true beliefs might have been useless or harmful false beliefs might have been useful. If we had been differently constituted, the utility of true and false beliefs might have been the reverse of what it is. This explanation leaves room for the possibility that human beings could have been wired in such a way that false beliefs directly produce useful behavior without causing intermediate true beliefs that in turn cause useful behavior. We could have been wired so that the false belief that wolves are vicious directly caused wolf-avoidance behavior. We could perhaps even have been wired in such a way that we tended to believe that the moon is made of cheese and that this belief caused us to avoid wolves.[1]

The pragmatic definition of truth paints quite a different picture. According to that theory, it could not have happened that true beliefs were not useful. We could not have been constructed in such a way that false beliefs were directly useful rather than true ones. All this follows from the nature of truth alone. If the belief that the moon is made of cheese happened to be useful, it would follow that it was also *true*. This is surely a counterintuitive consequence of pragmatism and may form the basis of an objection to the view. But our burden at this point is not to consider objections to pragmatism. It is to evaluate the arguments for pragmatism. And to object to the pragmatic argument, it is enough if there is an equally plausible competing explanation of the utility of true beliefs. It seems to me that our contingent explanation fits the bill. There is a fly in the ointment of the pragmatic argument.

The Epistemological Argument

One might aver that on pragmatism we can know the truth, whereas on the correspondence theory we cannot. This is the central claim of the epistemological argument for pragmatism. If truth is correspondence with facts that hold independently of us, then knowing the truth will require establishing such a correspondence. Yet, it might be claimed, there is no way to establish a correspondence with facts that hold independently of us. But if truth is what it is useful to believe, then knowing the truth requires only knowing that it is useful to believe certain propositions. And we are able to establish that certain beliefs are useful.

This is an epistemological argument similar in key respects to the epistemological arguments for idealism and relativism we have already mentioned and will again take up in Chapter 7. Nevertheless, new issues arise in the context of a theory of truth, and of pragmatism in particular, so it is worth entertaining the argument here. Let us begin by noting an ambiguity in the phrase "knowing the truth." This phrase may mean *knowing true propositions*, or it may mean *knowing that propositions are true*.

Suppose it means the former, knowing true propositions. The opponent of pragmatism may respond to the epistemological argument by denying that the correspondence theory and pragmatism differ in how difficult they make it to know a true proposition. For it is hard to see how theories of truth could bear on the difficulty of knowing true propositions. Theories of truth could bear on this matter only if knowing a true proposition were simply identified with knowing that the proposition is true. But that is an identity claim that a correspondence theorist and a pragmatist alike will abjure. Only a deflationist—one who says that by the definition of "true," <*p*> is true just in case *p*—could find such an identity claim attractive, and it isn't obviously correct even on deflationism, since it is not obvious that necessarily equivalent propositions can be substituted in the context "knows that" (e.g., it seems that one can know that the number of United States senators is one hundred without knowing that the number of senators is the square of ten, even though the first proposition is necessarily equivalent to the second). There are further arguments against the correspondence theory in this vicinity, but it is best to postpone them until Chapter 7. For now, it suffices to say that it is far from obvious how the correspondence theory could make knowing true propositions more costly than any other theory of truth does.

Suppose, in contrast, that knowing the truth means knowing that propositions are true. If a correspondence relation is, in large measure, a causal relation between the vehicle of representation (i.e., a belief or the usage of a sentence) and the objects represented—as it is on the correspondence theory I favor (see Chapter 6)—then knowing that a proposition is true is a matter of knowing that such a causal relation obtains. Knowing that a proposition is true is no more, and no less, difficult than knowing that certain causal relations obtain. But presumably everyone who is not a fairly radical skeptic will admit that it is possible to know causal relations of *some* kind. Certainly the pragmatist must admit this, since the utility of a belief is a matter of the causal consequences of the belief, so that one could scarcely know a belief's utility—hence know that the proposition believed is true—without knowing the causal consequences of the belief. Is it any more difficult to know the causal relations relevant to truth on the correspondence theory than to know those relevant to truth on pragmatism? I find it difficult to say.

According to the correspondence theory, I know that it is true that Napoleon lost at Waterloo only if I know that the name "Napoleon" is linked by usage to a historical figure who fought a certain battle and other things of this sort. Presumably to know this I must rely on testimony in a grand way, and so the plausibility of the correspondence theory depends on the epistemological power of testimony—a matter barely explored in epistemology (but see Coady 1992; Schmitt 1994b). Still, it is intuitively plausible that I can have such knowledge. By contrast, to know that it is true that Napoleon lost at Waterloo, on pragmatism, I must know the future causal consequences of believing that Napoleon lost at Waterloo, as well as the value of those consequences. But surely it is a tall order to judge what the consequences are or what value they have. I suppose the matter turns on such issues as the political lessons we may draw from Napoleon's loss and the bearing of those lessons on future politics. I, for one, am inclined to regard these issues as much more speculative and much harder to judge than the causal relations imposed by the correspondence theory. I doubt, therefore, that the pragmatist is in a position to press the epistemological argument against the correspondence theory.

We have considered two arguments for pragmatism. Neither carries the day for the pragmatist.

III. Objections to the Pragmatic Theory of Truth

There are numerous serious objections to pragmatism. The view suffers from counterexamples of two sorts. It is also encumbered by a commitment to relativism and a certain kind of incoherence.

Useful False Beliefs Objection

Pragmatism, as we have so far formulated it, is patently false (Lovejoy 1908, Russell 1967). For there are glaring counterexamples. The proposition that wolves are vicious is a false proposition that it is useful to believe. At least, belief in that proposition could be useful for anyone who came into contact with wolves in the wild. And arguably for such people the proposition would be more useful to believe than not to believe. Moreover, it would be more useful to believe the proposition than to believe its negation (at any rate, this would be so if one would not steer clear of wolves unless one believed wolves to be vicious). It might even be that, for most of us, it is more useful to believe the proposition than to believe the *true* proposition that wolves are dangerous. For the former belief is more likely to motivate us (and it is likely to motivate us more powerfully) to avoid wolves than is belief in the latter. Thus, there are useful false beliefs, and the pragmatist is simply wrong to identify true propositions with those it is useful to believe.

Nor will it avail the pragmatist to reply to the counterexample by revising the theory to say that true propositions are the ones useful for *everyone* (or for most people) to believe. To be sure, the proposition that wolves are vicious is not useful for *everyone* to believe. Not everyone meets up with wolves in the wild. And so this mixed theory no longer entails that the proposition is true. The problem, however, is that the revised condition on truth is too strong: few true propositions are universally useful to believe. Moreover, there are propositions that are or have been useful for most people to believe for which we nevertheless lack any temptation to infer from their utility that they are true. For many people, it is useful to believe in God or in the afterlife, but we would not infer from this fact that belief in God or the afterlife is true.

Thus, pragmatism as formulated is flatly mistaken. Might it be reformulated to avoid the objection? Note that pragmatism may avail itself of our earlier point that, in general, when a false belief is useful, it is useful either because one infers a true belief from it or because it causes one to believe a truth. The pragmatist may answer the objection by distinguishing beliefs that are useful *directly* from beliefs that are useful *indirectly*.

> A belief is useful *indirectly* when it is useful only because one *infers* another useful belief from it or because it *causes* one to hold another useful belief.
>
> A belief is useful *directly* when it is useful but *not* indirectly useful.

Now the pragmatist may define the true propositions as the ones belief in which is *directly* useful. Clearly, there are falsehoods belief in which is *indirectly* useful—e.g., the falsehood that wolves are vicious. The pragmatist must concede this point, but it is no objection to the new, more guarded version of pragmatism. And it is not obvious that there are any falsehoods belief in which is *directly* useful. If there are no such falsehoods, then the useful false proposition counterexamples to pragmatism fall away.

Does the new, guarded pragmatism evade all the useful false proposition counterexamples to the original version? It is not easy to say, and I will not attempt to judge the matter here. It seems to me that the reply has at least the *prospect* of success. But, unfortunately for the pragmatist, even if the useful false proposition counterexamples to pragmatism evaporate, other counterexamples remain. In particular, even if there are no actually directly useful false propositions, it is nevertheless *possible* for there to be directly useful false beliefs. We *could* have been so constituted and situated that false beliefs directly cause useful actions. Yet pragmatism entails that necessarily, false beliefs are useless. So pragmatism is mistaken.

The pragmatist might try to get around the latter counterexamples by making pragmatism say that the false beliefs in a possible world are not the ones that are useless for creatures to believe as they are constituted and situated in that world, but the ones that it would be useless for *us* to believe if we were in that world but constituted and situated as we are in the *real* world. I suspect that this proposal gets into a peck of trouble, but we need not judge its success. Other counterexamples to pragmatism seem to me harder to handle.

Useless True Beliefs Objection

There are innumerable truths it is useless to believe. For example, there are useless truths about the precise temperature of small regions in the interior of certain stars that are unknown to us. For that matter, there are useless truths about the precise temperature of small regions in the interior of my desk. Believing these truths is no more useful than believing their negations. This shows that pragmatism goes awry in its implication that whenever a proposition is true, it is useful to believe it.

It is hard to see how the pragmatist could circumvent this objection except by insisting that though these truths are not *now* useful to *us*, they *could be* useful to *someone* at *some* time. This would, however, require a new pragmatic account of truth:

> <*p*> is true just in case believing *p* could be useful to someone at some time.

The trouble with this new account is that we can imagine circumstances and beings for whom it would be useful to believe *falsehoods*. We can imagine beings for whom it would be useful to believe that wolves are vicious—indeed, useful because this belief would cause them to avoid wolves *without* their inferring any useful truth from this belief. In other words, if the pragmatist now says that the truths are the propositions that it could be useful for someone to believe at some time, then the objection is that, for any falsehood, we can always imagine circumstances and beings for whom it would be useful to believe that falsehood. The pragmatist might propose that truths are propositions it could be useful for an *ideal* being to believe, where an ideal being is one who would not avoid wolves without inferring that they are dangerous from the belief that they are vicious. To be sure, the pragmatist could, if possessed of infinite intellectual resources, define for each true proposition an ideal being for whom belief in the proposition would be useful. But why hold out hope of defining a *single* kind of ideal being for whom true propositions are all useful to believe? It is hard to imagine any one kind of ideal being for whom every truth would be useful to believe.

Relativism Objection

Pragmatism may be criticized for its commitment to *relativism* about truth. As we have already noted, what it is useful to believe varies from culture to culture, individual to individual, and circumstance to circumstance. It may be useful to believe a proposition in one circumstance and useful not to believe it or to believe its negation in another circumstance. What it is useful to believe depends on one's background beliefs, desires, and environment, and all these things vary widely from culture to culture.

Now, some differences in what it is useful for people in different cultures to believe do not require relativizing pragmatic truth to different systems of belief. For example, it might be useful for a Western physicist to believe that $E = mc^2$, but it might not be useful for a Senegalese villager to believe this. The pragmatist may handle such differences by compiling all the propositions it is useful for anyone to believe: let the true propositions be the set of all propositions it is useful for anyone to believe. This set of propositions may not be very tidy or coherent, but then it is hardly obvious that the truth is very coherent either.

The need to relativize pragmatic truth arises, rather, when it is useful for a person in one culture to believe a proposition and useful for a person in another culture to believe its negation. It could be useful in general for Italians to believe in original sin, but useful in general for the Japanese to disbelieve in it. Hence, on pragmatism, truth varies from culture to culture in such a way that a proposition can be true relative to one culture and its negation true relative to another. Pragmatism is committed to relativism. But, the objection continues, relativism is at least mistaken and perhaps downright incoherent, for the reasons given in Chapter 2. Hence, pragmatism is mistaken.

One way to respond to this objection is to make the pragmatic theory *indexical* rather than relativistic. That is, the pragmatist may say that the subject for whom belief in a true proposition is useful is the truth-*ascriber*. Usefulness is indexical in the sense that it implicitly refers to the truth-ascriber. (So understood, pragmatism joins the issue between the correspondence theory and deflationism: whether truth involves a relation to a truth-ascriber. We will discuss this issue in Chapters 5 and 6.) Such an indexical pragmatic theory is *not* relativistic; it does not entail that one and the same proposition is true relative to one subject and false relative to another. When one ascriber says that a proposition is true and another says that it is not, the two ascribers are not at all contradicting one another. Rather, one is saying that it is useful for *her* to believe it and the other is saying that it is useful for *him* to believe it. There is no contradiction at all between these claims. This move to ascriber-indexicality also avoids the meaning and regress objections that plagued relativism—a point I will leave to the reader to verify. Thus, the indexical theory has considerable advantages over the stock unindexed version of pragmatism. Unfortunately, the advantages are purchased at the cost of implausibility. For it is surely the case that when one person says that a proposition is true and another denies it, they *do* contradict each other. The indexical version of pragmatism runs afoul of the commonplace that truth-talk is used to disagree.

A more promising way for the pragmatist to respond to the relativism objection is to identify the truths with the propositions it is *directly* useful to believe, as in the earlier response to the counterexamples to pragmatism. It is unclear that it is *directly* useful in general for Italians to believe in original sin and for the Japanese to believe that there is no original sin. If the Italian belief in original sin is useful because, say, it causes people to believe the truth that forgiveness of others is a virtue, then there need be no conflict between the proposition it is *directly* useful for Italians to believe here and the proposition it is directly useful for the Japanese to believe. The pragmatist who responds in this way to the relativism objection is gambling that it will never turn out that there are inconsistent directly useful beliefs across cultures.

This is not a silly gamble. For the reason why pragmatism appears to give rise to relativism is that background beliefs and conditions make contrary beliefs useful. If the fact that contrary beliefs are useful in different cultures can be explained by a difference in what it is directly useful to believe in those cultures, and the propositions it is directly useful to believe are not themselves contraries, then the pragmatist may respond to the relativist objection by making truth what it is directly useful to believe. No inconsistencies across cultures will then arise, and pragmatic truth need not be relativized to cultures.

It is, again, exceedingly difficult to evaluate this response, and so we must leave the outcome of the relativism objection to pragmatism inconclusive.

Regress Objection

Quite apart from whether pragmatism entails relativism, it faces an objection closely analogous to the third, regress, objection to relativism discussed in Chapter 2. The right-hand side of the pragmatist definition of truth—it is useful to believe that *p*—is a proposition about the usefulness of belief. But if it is useful to believe *p*, then surely its being useful to believe *p* determines (in part) that it is *true* that it is useful to believe *p*. In general, if *q*, then (as I will put it) its being the case that *q* determines that *q* is true. Its being useful to believe *q* does not. But then the pragmatist must admit that pragmatism is mistaken in application to a great many propositions—all propositions *q* of the form <it is useful to believe *p*>. For pragmatism says that what determines that *q* is true is not its being the case that *q* but its being useful to believe *q*. Moreover, pragmatism must be mistaken in application to propositions not of the form <it is useful to believe *p*>. For beliefs are useful or useless in virtue of their relation to desires, actions, and environments: *S*'s belief is useful in an environment if it enables *S* to satisfy *S*'s desires in that environment. So for a belief to be useful, there have to be desires, actions, and environments with certain properties. But once these entities—desires, actions, and environments—are admitted, it must surely also be admitted that what makes propositions about them true is (at least in part) what is the case concerning them, *not* what it is useful to believe about them. So pragmatism runs aground here. The difficulty is quite parallel to the difficulty facing transcendental idealism, that the view depends on an implausible ontological dualism between minds and bodies. Here pragmatism is charged with an implausible dualism between what it is useful to believe and other states of affairs.

Might the pragmatist be saved from catastrophe by admitting that what it is useful to believe is determined by desires, actions, and environments, but at the same time insisting that this admission is not to be taken as allowing that anything is the case concerning whether a belief is useful? Might the pragmatist say instead that pragmatism is to be taken as relativizing whether it is useful to believe *p* to a background condition—namely, to the background condition of what it is useful to believe? Then whether <*p*> is true is determined by whether it is useful to believe *p*, and that is determined, not by desires, actions, and environments, but rather relative to what it is useful for someone to believe regarding desires, actions, and environments. The trouble with this move should be clear: it can stave off the world only if it is carried out ad infinitum. If it stops at any point, then there is a world, and what is true must then be determined by what is the case, not by what it is useful to believe. But if the move is carried out forever, then pragmatism will assign *no* particular truth-values to propositions, even relative truth-values. Yet the point of a theory of truth is to fix truth-values.

There seems to be only one other response open to the pragmatist: embrace a version of idealism on which, for any proposition *q* that makes trouble in the manner described, the state of affairs that *q* is nothing other than (or at least a part of) its being useful to believe *q*. But this is surely no more plausible for the troublesome propositions than it is for any other proposition. Consider another sort of proposition, say <Snow is white>. The state of affairs snow's being white is surely not the state of affairs its being useful to believe that snow is white. And neither is the state of affairs its being useful to believe *p* identical with the state of affairs its being useful to believe that it is useful to believe *p*. The regress objection seems to me as lethal to pragmatism as its twin was to relativism.

It is an interesting question how far this objection to pragmatism generalizes to other theories of truth. I'll stick my neck out and suggest that it shows the implausibility of all descriptivist theories of truth (i.e., all theories of truth that define truth in descriptive language) other than deflationism and the correspondence theory. Suppose one claims that "<*p*> is true" is to be defined as "<*p*> has property *X*." Where <*p*> is true, this entails that it is the case that <*p*> has *X*. But if <*p*> has *X*, then <*p*>'s having *X* in large part (if not entirely) makes true the proposition < <*p*> has *X*>. It does not make true the proposition <*p*>, *unless* the state of affairs that *p* is nothing other than (or at least is a large part of) <*p*>'s having *X*. There are few *X*'s for which this will be so. The problem is not that the *X* identified by pragmatism (or by other theories) is not extensionally adequate in the sense that necessarily, when *p*, <*p*> has *X*. Suppose *X is* extensionally adequate. Even so, having *X* will plausibly enter into making <*p*> true only for a very few choices of *X*, once it is admitted that *p*. The problem, in a nutshell, is that once you have it that *p*, you don't need much of an *X*. Its being the case that *p* gives us most, if not all, of what we need for <*p*> to be true. The only proposed descriptivist theories of truth that sit with this result are deflationism (which sits very well with it indeed) and the correspondence theory (which sits a bit less comfortably with it, since the theory adds something to its being the case that *p*). I am inclined, therefore, to regard the regress objection as repelling us not only from pragmatism but also from virtually any view other than deflationism or the correspondence theory, at least as long as we regard truth as having a definition in descriptive language.

Epistemological Objection

There is one last objection to pragmatism, related to our response to the epistemological argument for pragmatism and in some ways an epistemological analogue of the regress objection: pragmatism misgauges our knowledge of truth (Russell 1910). Here knowledge of truth is knowledge that given propositions are true. On pragmatism, to know that a proposition *p* is true is to know whether it is useful to believe that *p*. The trouble with this is that when we seek to know whether it is true that, say, snow is white, we do not ask whether it is useful to believe this proposition. The latter inquiry would have us explore the behavioral consequences of believing the proposition. But when we seek to know whether the proposition is true, we ask an entirely different question: whether snow is as described in the proposition. That involves examining snow and its properties. It has no obvious connection with the usefulness of believing the proposition.

This objection is compelling against the pragmatism we have dealt with in this chapter, which makes truth a matter of the behavioral and cognitive usefulness of belief. This or a like objection, however, propelled Lovejoy and Russell to suggest that James must really have had in mind a *cognitive* rather than a behavioral version of pragmatism. If truth is a matter of the *cognitive* rather than behavioral utility of belief, and cognitive utility is the capacity of a belief to organize, predict, and explain experience, then the pragmatist may say that to judge whether it is true that snow is white, we must gauge our reasons for belief in that proposition, and that is a matter of judging the ability of the belief to organize, predict, and explain our experience. Thus, judging whether a proposition is true does embroil us in judging whether it is cognitively useful to believe it. A cognitive pragmatism, it might be said, does not launch us on a wild goose chase in judging whether propositions are true as a behavioral pragmatism does, but rather nudges us in just the right direction.

It is no easy matter to measure the success of this response. For the objector might maintain that the cognitive pragmatist still misgauges our knowledge of truth. To judge whether <snow is white> is true, we must of course *have* reasons for belief. But we need not judge whether we have these reasons. Our attention is turned toward snow and its properties, not toward the presence of reasons. Or at least we need not judge these reasons. I am inclined to regard this objection as forceful, though I recognize that the pragmatist could always return with the insistence that even in perceptual knowledge, we must judge the reasons. (It is worth adding that, whatever its prospects against the epistemological objection, cognitive pragmatism makes no headway against the useful true and useless false counterexamples nor against the relativism or vagueness objections, though other epistemic theories of truth may handle comparable counterexamples.)

The objections to pragmatism we have canvassed, at least the useless true belief and regress objections, mount a formidable case against the pragmatic theory of truth. Let us note in connection with the fundamental matter of whether truth involves a relation to thinkers that all of the objections to pragmatism bear on this matter. All the objections we have covered are designed to show that, intuitively, truth does not involve a relation to thinkers in the manner pragmatism proclaims. Thus, the objections, in so far as they succeed, point us away from a conception of truth that makes it a relation to thinkers (other, perhaps, than the relatively innocuous relation between believer and fact entailed by the correspondence theory, at least when beliefs are the bearers of truth-value). The regress objection to pragmatism, moreover, seems to favor adopting either deflationism or the correspondence theory over alternatives. We will, however, have to look at the coherence theory for a final judgment on that matter.

IV. The Pragmatic Theory of Meaning

We have dwelt on the pragmatic theory of truth. I would like to close this chapter with a word about the pragmatic theory of meaning and its bearing on truth.

The pragmatic theory of meaning concerns the content of our concepts. It tells us when concepts are identical. In particular, it makes concept identity an epistemological matter:

> The concept of *F* is identical with the concept of *G* just in case we cannot distinguish *F*s from *G*s.

The pragmatic theory of meaning defines concept identity in terms of our being unable to distinguish *F*s from *G*s—an epistemological matter. (There is a precisely analogous account of when the terms "*F* " and "*G*" have the same meaning.) This account of concept identity bears a close resemblance to the later verificationist theory of meaning of the Viennese logical positivists, according to which the meaning of a sentence is its method of verification: two sentences have the same meaning when we would employ the same means of verifying sentences. The pragmatic account of concept identity also bears a resemblance, albeit a more distant one, to justification-condition theories of meaning, which hold that the meaning of sentences is given not by their truth-conditions but by their justification-conditions, the conditions under which they are justified (Pollock 1974, Dummett 1978). (We will examine a justification-condition theory of truth in the next chapter.) For our purposes of understanding the pragmatic theory of meaning and its relation to the pragmatic theory of truth, we need not explore the relation between these theories of meaning.

How are the pragmatic theories of meaning and truth related? Although Peirce and James both adhere to the pragmatic theory of meaning, the theories of truth they propose are in fact inconsistent with this theory. The pragmatic theory of meaning would identify the concept of truth with the concept of something indistinguishable from truth. Presumably, however, *F*s are indistinguishable from *G*s when, after our best cognitive effort, we would believe something to be *F* if we were to believe it to be *G* and vice versa. But after our best cognitive effort, we would believe a proposition to be true if we were to believe it to be justified for us, and vice versa. So truth is indistinguishable from justified belief (for discussion, see Neely forthcoming). Thus, on the pragmatic theory of meaning, the concept of truth must be the concept of justified belief.

In practice, however, Peirce and James do not identify the concept of truth with that of justified belief. They identify it with other concepts altogether. For James, as we have seen, the concept of truth is the concept of what it is useful to believe, while for Peirce, as we will see in the next chapter, it is the concept of belief that would result from the proper method of inquiry if that method were carried out to its limit—until all the beliefs resulting from it were stable and none were ever retracted. However, these conditions—of the usefulness of belief and of the limit of inquiry—are distinguishable from truth. Thus, the pragmatic theory of meaning is inconsistent with the Peircean and Jamesian theories of truth.

One could of course observe that even though we cannot distinguish the truth from our own justified beliefs, we can distinguish it from the justified beliefs of others. Moreover, we recognize that it is possible for our own justified beliefs to be false. This does show that the concept of truth is not the concept of justified belief. But the pragmatic theory of meaning has no way to recognize any of this. It cannot accommodate the first point, that we can distinguish the truth from the justified beliefs of others, since indistinguishability is always relative to a subject. Our concept of truth is indistinguishability *for us*, and we cannot distinguish the truth from our justified beliefs. Of course, if no one could be justified in a belief unless all others were justified as well, then it could not happen that we distinguish the truth from the justified beliefs of others. But this is not true of our concept of justified belief. Nor will it help to make the truth what is justified for all cognizers as a group, since the group of all cognizers could still distinguish the truth from what some members are justified in believing—at least they could if what is justified for the group were not necessarily what is justified for each member (as I argue in Schmitt 1994c). The pragmatic theory of meaning cannot honor the most intuitive features of our concept of truth.

I speculate that Peirce was driven to his conception of truth by his commitment to the pragmatic theory of meaning and its consequence that the concept of truth is the concept of justified belief. But as a philosopher endowed with as much common sense as brilliant imagination, Peirce could not rest with the identity of truth and justified belief. Moreover, he recognized that it would not help to identify the concept of truth with the concept of some future justified beliefs; for any justified beliefs we will or could have could also be false. Peirce accordingly settled for identifying the concept of truth with the concept of *ideally* justified belief—the output of the proper method taken to its limit. But this theory of truth is inconsistent with the pragmatic theory of meaning.

The reasoning we have just been through shows that the pragmatic theory of meaning must be rejected; it cannot accommodate our concept of truth. One who wishes to preserve the gist of the pragmatic theory of meaning must therefore find a way to restrict it. To do so, one might limit the theory to apply only to *useful* concepts. There is no use, it might be said, in having a concept of truth identical with a concept other than that of justified belief, since we cannot distinguish truth from justified belief. It would then be claimed that the concept of truth is useless. Of course, this admission, and the restricted pragmatic theory of meaning that entails it, are hostage to any discovery that the concept of truth *is* useful. Thus, the linguistic argument for deflationism already discussed and the arguments for the correspondence theory of truth we will discuss in Chapter 6 speak directly against this restricted pragmatic theory of meaning. If these arguments are successful, then the concept of truth is useful even though it violates the pragmatic theory of meaning. Thus, to the extent that these arguments persuade us, and given that the best defense of the pragmatic theory of meaning is the restricted version, we must reject the pragmatic theory of meaning altogether. Neither the pragmatic theory of truth nor the pragmatic theory of meaning is left standing.

In this chapter, we have considered a simple pragmatic theory of truth. We have examined two arguments for the theory—the pragmatic argument and the epistemological argument—and found them both wanting. We have also entertained a raft of objections to pragmatism. There are two sorts of counterexamples to the pragmatic theory of truth—useful false beliefs and useless true beliefs. The former may be and the latter certainly is a menace to pragmatism. Pragmatism may entail relativism and in any case suffers from a regress problem analogous to the regress that obstructs relativism. And there is an epistemological objection to pragmatism. These objections urge us to abandon the idea that truth is a relation to believers in the manner described by pragmatism. In light of all this, I feel warranted in proclaiming the view moribund.

Chapter Four

The Coherence Theory

The pragmatic theory of truth is one theory that makes truth a relation between propositions and believers. Truth, on the pragmatic theory, involves an interesting and deep relation to believers. In this regard, the pragmatic theory is in league with relativism and at variance with the correspondence theory of truth. The failure of the pragmatic theory of truth will encourage those inclined to maintain that truth involves such an interesting and deep relation to believers to try a *coherence* theory of truth.

On a coherence theory, a true proposition is one that belongs to some designated coherent set of propositions. The designated set is typically defined epistemologically, in which case the coherence theory is one of a broader class of theories, *epistemic* theories of truth—theories that define truth in terms of epistemic justification or knowledge. The designated set may, however, be defined ontologically. We will touch on the ontological interpretation but focus on the epistemological. Both versions of the coherence theory make truth a deep relation to believers. But the epistemological version, and indeed all epistemic theories of truth, go beyond this in making truth wholly dependent on and in some sense constituted by the mind. In this regard, they go considerably beyond the pragmatic theory. For the pragmatic theory makes truth only partly dependent on, and only tenuously constituted by, the mind. Thus, the epistemological version of the coherence theory and other epistemic theories of truth more closely parallel ontological idealism than the pragmatic theory does.

The coherence theory of truth has been imputed to philosophers as diverse as J. G. Fichte, G. W. F. Hegel, F. H. Bradley, and Brand Blanshard. The view is sometimes traced to Immanuel Kant and before him to Baruch Spinoza (Walker 1989, 48-60). It must be admitted, however, that these figures present very different conceptions of truth and reality, and I wonder whether lumping them together as adherents of the coherence theory of truth does not blur rather than clarify their views. I will accordingly avoid interpreting these figures and instead examine two ways in which a coherence theory of truth might naturally arise.

We may define the coherence theory of truth as the view that truth is coherence—membership in a coherent set of actual or ideal beliefs. For the moment, we may ride on this bare-bones version of the theory:

> <*p*> is true just in case <*p*> belongs to a designated coherent set of propositions.

(Alternatively, it might be said that <*p*> is true just in case <*p*> coheres with a designated set of propositions. I will, for convenience, stick with the first formulation.)

Everything turns of course on what the terms "coherent" and "designated" mean. These terms must be defined in such a way as to generate the properties of truth. To see how the terms might be defined, let us review the arguments for a coherence theory of truth.

I. Arguments for the Coherence Theory

The Internal Relations Argument

One argument for a coherence theory of truth adverts to an ontological claim, the doctrine of internal relations (Blanshard 1941, 316). What is required, on the standard version of the argument, is a strong version of the doctrine of internal relations. It will, however, help to look first at a weak version of this doctrine: no object would be what it intrinsically is, nor would it even exist, if other objects did not exist and bear the relations to it they do. An object would not be a mountain, say, and would not even exist if it did not bear relations to a valley as well as to all other objects. The required stronger version of the doctrine of internal relations would hold that an object is what it is in virtue of its place or function in the totality of objects. An alligator is nothing but a thing that bears certain relations to other things. (The strong doctrine of internal relations is akin to the functionalism about objects described in Chapter 1.)

Now, the internal relations argument proceeds this way. From this strong doctrine of internal relations, one might infer that what it is for an object to exist or have a certain property is for its having that property to cohere in a sense with other objects having other properties. The object's having the property must cohere in the sense that the object bears the relations to other objects in virtue of which it has the property. Consequently, what it is for the proposition that the object has the property to be *true* is for this proposition to cohere with propositions to the effect that other objects have other properties. In other words, the strong doctrine of internal relations entails the coherence theory of truth. (I will remark momentarily on whether the weak doctrine might also be taken to establish the coherence theory.)

This internal relations argument for the coherence theory is unconvincing even granting the strong doctrine of internal relations. Even if that doctrine is true—even if an object has a property only if it bears certain relations to other objects—it does not follow that the *truth* of the proposition that the object has that property consists in the proposition's coherence with other propositions. To see this, note that the first step in the argument assumes equivalences of the form: <*p*> is true just in case *p*. But the argument furnishes no reason for saying that truth is defined by coherence rather than by these equivalences (as on a deflationary theory of truth—see Chapter 5) or by some other theory of truth that entails the equivalences. Thus the argument supplies no reason for converting an ontological doctrine, the strong doctrine of internal relations, to a semantical one, the coherence theory of truth.

Note as well that if the argument did prevail, its conclusion could be established without appeal to the strong or even the weak doctrine of internal relations. The strong doctrine entails that in all possible situations a given object has a property in virtue of bearing the *same* relations to other objects. But all that is needed to establish the coherence theory of truth is that in all possible situations a given object has a property in virtue of bearing some relation *or other* to other objects. These relations need not be the same in all possible situations. All that is necessary for the argument is that the proposition that the object has the property is true in virtue of coherence—i.e., in virtue of bearing relations to other propositions. If the internal relations argument for the coherence theory were successful, the doctrine of internal relations would be dispensable for purposes of establishing the coherence theory of truth. Of course, I deny that the argument is successful.

The Epistemological Argument

There is, however, another sort of argument for the coherence theory with a greater prospect of success, one that adverts to an epistemological rather than an ontological claim. The idea is to derive the coherence theory of truth from a coherence theory of justification. This argument is perhaps most explicit in Blanshard (1941, 260-265). The argument bears some resemblance to the epistemological arguments for idealism and pragmatism, but it raises special issues of its own, so I will treat it here in some detail.

The impetus behind the epistemological argument is that justification and truth are essentially tied. Justification is conceived as the test or criterion of truth—our means of judging the truth. To be sure, truth extends beyond justification—there are truths that no one is justified in believing. But truth is naturally conceived as an *extension* of justification. Hence, truth is to be defined in terms of justification. But justification is coherence. So, the argument concludes, truth is coherence.

To scan the argument more slowly, we are to assume a coherence theory of justification. That is,

> A subject *S* is justified in believing that *p* just in case <*p*> belongs to a designated set of propositions belief in which is coherent for *S*.

The argument then claims that a coherence theory of justification entails a coherence theory of truth. For justification is the test or criterion of truth: justification is a property of a proposition that enables the subject to judge or determine whether the proposition is true. But something is a test or criterion of a property *P* only if an object's passing the test guarantees that it has property *P*. Hence, something is a test of truth only if a proposition that meets the test is guaranteed to be true. But then, since justification is coherence, a coherent proposition must be guaranteed to be true. Thus, truth is coherence. In sum, the coherence theory of justification entails the coherence theory of truth. Once we accept the coherence theory of justification, we should also accept the coherence theory of truth.[1]

The epistemological argument puts an important constraint on the coherence theory of truth. It entails that, necessarily, justified propositions (or, as we may say, assuming the coherence theory of justification, propositions that are justification-coherent) are true.[2] So the coherence required by truth—"truth-coherence," for short—must be defined in such a way that all justification-coherent propositions are truth-coherent. Truth-coherence will presumably be identical with justification-coherence for justified propositions. Of course this leaves open just what truth-coherence amounts to for propositions that are not justified.

All this suggests a simple strategy for developing a coherence theory of truth. The coherentist begins with justification-coherence. Truth is identified with justification-coherence for justified propositions. The coherentist about truth then defines truth-coherence for other propositions by extending justification-coherence in some natural way beyond the arena of justified propositions. There are, intuitively, many true propositions besides the ones that are justified—e.g., propositions about the local temperatures of the interior of a star we have never observed. The set of propositions justified for human subjects is indeed tiny in comparison with the set of truths. For the set of truths is nearly complete—for any proposition $<p>$, $<p>$ is either true or false, with the exception of borderline vague propositions (see Chapter 5) and perhaps certain other troublesome propositions (such as those involved in the semantical paradoxes like the liar paradox). But the set of justified propositions is nowhere near complete.

To remedy this implication of incompleteness, the coherentist might add propositions to the set of justified propositions in this way: given a proposition <*p*> such that neither <*p*> nor <not-*p*> is justified for *S*, add <*p*> to the designated set when the resulting set of propositions would continue to justification-cohere for *S*. In this way, the coherentist may build up a nearly complete set of propositions. The designated coherent set of propositions would then be the initial set of justified propositions together with all those propositions that are added in the manner described. By identifying the true propositions with those in this designated coherent set, the coherentist offers a nearly complete set of truths and thus answers the incompleteness objection.

Is the epistemological argument for the coherence theory of truth persuasive? I will limit myself to one obvious gripe: a test of a property *P* need not guarantee that an object that passes the test has *P*. Litmus paper provides a test of acid, but it does not guarantee that a liquid that tests positive is an acid. Similarly, a test of truth need not guarantee truth. But then, even if justification is the test of truth and justification is coherence, not every coherent belief need be true. The epistemological argument no longer establishes that truth is coherence.

Might the proponent of the epistemological argument retrench and assume only that the test of truth must *generally* pick out a true proposition? Then the argument will entail only that justified propositions are *generally* true. This argument would lead to a version of the coherence theory of truth on which true propositions are defined, not as justification-coherent propositions, but as some idealization thereof.

The proposal to idealize justified propositions has some promise. We will consider whether idealizing justification may save the day in Sections II and III below. Meanwhile, we should spy a weakness in the epistemological argument. I am partial to the argument's assumption that justification is the test of truth and that justified beliefs must generally be true. But these assumptions sit poorly with the coherence theory of justification. If justification is (by necessity) the test of truth, then it is not plausibly identified with coherent belief. For there could be a justification-coherent fantasy—a set of justification-coherent propositions that are not generally true. If one accepts the assumption that justification is the test of truth, as I do, one should reject the coherence theory of justification. The price of doing so, however, is losing the epistemological argument.

The contemporary theory of justification that fits best with the classical assumption that justification is the test of truth is *reliabilism*: justified belief is belief formed by a process that tends to form true beliefs (Goldman 1986, Schmitt 1992). Reliabilism makes the link between justification and truth *necessary*, as the view that justification is the test of truth requires. The coherence theory of justification, in contrast, breaks the necessary connection between justification and truth. The premise that justification is coherence retains its intuitive appeal only on a conception of justification on which justification is *not* the test of truth. So the epistemological argument packs no punch. The coherence theory of justification not only does not entail a coherence theory of truth; it is inconsistent with it.[3]

II. Objections to the Coherence Theory

We may lodge several complaints about the coherence theory of truth, as it emerges from the epistemological argument.

Justified False Propositions Objection

One problem with the coherence theory of truth, already broached above, applies to any theory of truth that makes justified propositions true: justified propositions can, intuitively, be false and even inconsistent. A subject can, for example, be justified in believing that at least one of his or her beliefs is false. In such a case, it is *guaranteed* that the propositions justified for the subject are inconsistent, since the proposition that at least one of a set of beliefs is false is inconsistent with the conjunction of propositions in the set. Moreover, to make a different observation that is also pertinent here, a proposition can be justified for one subject and its negation justified for another subject, so that truth cannot be what is justified for *both* subjects. So justified propositions can be false.

The coherentist may handle the problem of inconsistency *across* subjects by relativizing truth to individual subjects. But of course that lands the coherentist in the briar patch of relativism, with its thicket of difficulties (see Chapter 2). And relativizing does not help the problem of inconsistent and false propositions justified for a *single* subject.

To handle within-subject inconsistencies, the coherentist must, as intimated above, idealize justified propositions so as to purge false propositions and inconsistencies within and across subjects—e.g., by making the truths the propositions belonging to the most coherent of the consistent subsets of the initial set of propositions justified for all subjects. The trouble is that coherentism cannot by itself eliminate the indeterminacies to which this idealization is heir. There is always more than one way to purge a set of propositions of inconsistencies. If two propositions, p and q, are inconsistent, one can purge p or instead purge q. The coherentist might try to reduce this indeterminacy by placing further constraints on the purged set of propositions—for example, letting the truths be the most coherent consistent subset containing the *most information* (in the sense that it has the most content). But even this constraint will not necessarily determine a unique set of truths, since there could always be two most coherent subsets with maximal information. Of course the coherentist could have us arbitrarily choose one set to be the true set. But surely it is counterintuitive to suppose that truth is arbitrary in this way.

In addition to this problem of indeterminacy, there is also the point that there is no reason to suppose that purging inconsistencies will eliminate justified but false beliefs. It seems that the coherentist will have to employ radical measures to eliminate these.

Justified Propositions Unstable Objection

Before we turn our attention to these radical measures, we should note one other objection to the coherence theory of truth. Propositions justified for a subject at a certain time may cease to be justified in light of further evidence the subject acquires. I may at first be justified in believing that a distant tower is round, but as I approach, I see it more clearly and judge that it is square; I come to be justified in believing that it is square. Justified propositions are not stable. But, according to the skeptic, propositions at one time true do not cease to be true; they are stable. So, the objection concludes, truth cannot be justification.

To answer this objection, the coherentist might allow propositions to count as true only when they retain their justification over time. I will return to this suggestion below.

III. Other Epistemic Theories of Truth

Let us move now to epistemic theories of truth, theories that promise to circumvent both objection (1) and objection (2) to the coherence theory. Virtually all epistemic theories of truth forgo the resources of the coherence theory of justification and treat truth as idealized justification. In particular, these theories identify truth with the *limit of justification*: let the true propositions be those which would be justified in the limit of inquiry.

Here are three epistemic theories that make truth the limit of justification. On one theory, truth is said to be justification under the *totality of all possible evidence*:

> <*p*> is true just in case <*p*> is justified after all possible evidence has been taken into account.

A second theory is *C. S. Peirce's*:

> <*p*> is true just in case belief that *p* would result from the proper method of inquiry applied until all beliefs that result from the method are stable.

On Peirce's theory, a true proposition is one that results from the proper method—i.e., would not be revised by that method as a result of further use of the method in light of whatever experiences inquirers would have. The proper method of inquiry, for Peirce, is the method that tends to stabilize beliefs.

A third epistemic theory has been suggested by Crispin Wright (1992, 44-70) to serve as an account of the truth of propositions on certain topics, though Wright does not go so far as to endorse the theory. According to this theory, truth is *superjustification*:

> <*p*> is true just in case <*p*> is justified by some amount of evidence and remains justified no matter what further evidence is added to the original evidence.

I will assume that the evidence referred to here is possible evidence—evidence that could be acquired by a physically and cognitively unlimited inquirer—and not just evidence actually possessed by or available to some actual subject. Without this assumption, the present theory would succumb to an objection analogous to objection (2) to pragmatism: there are true propositions for which no evidence will ever be available (e.g., about the local temperatures of the interior of unobserved stars).

The Peircean and superjustification theories have an advantage over the totality of evidence theory: they do not entail that there is a totality of all possible evidence (see also Ellis 1969). I will not, however, make much of the difference between these accounts, and for convenience I will focus on the superjustification account. The other theories face quite similar objections.

Uniqueness Objection

The following state of affairs seems possible: that a proposition and its negation are both justified by some amount of evidence for different subjects and remain so no matter what evidence is added to this original evidence. Indeed, there will be such propositions if there is *underdetermination* of theories of a certain kind. Suppose there are competing theories underdetermined by all possible evidence—theories consistent with and equally supported by all possible evidence. Suppose also that subjects may nevertheless be justified in believing different competing theories. This would happen, most plausibly, if the subjects held contrary but justified views as to which theory is favored by theoretical desiderata, and these views could affect the justification of the theories. (An extreme empiricist would deny that this could happen, insisting that when competing theories are equally supported by the evidence, we must suspend judgment between them. But, as I will note below, an empiricist of this sort would either have to accept that there are true theories that are not superjustified—in which case the superjustification theory is mistaken—or accept an implausible verificationist theory of meaning, on which there could be no distinct theories underdetermined by all possible evidence.) If justification in the face of underdetermination of the kind just described is possible, then it can happen that <*p*> is superjustified and at the same time a contrary proposition <*q*> is too. Since either <*p*> is false or <*q*> is false, it follows that a false proposition can be superjustified, contrary to the superjustification theory. To put the point differently, the superjustification theory rules out the possibility of the sort of underdetermination described.

Yet it seems that such underdetermination is possible. At least, there is nothing of an epistemological nature to rule it out. It is often the case that one theory is preferred to a second theory on grounds other than evidence. For example, the Copernican theory of planetary motion was preferred to the Ptolemaic theory on grounds of simplicity and explanatory power, even though it saved the evidence less well than the latter theory. If this is so, then it is hard to see why one theory might not be preferred to a second, competing theory on grounds of simplicity and explanatory power, even though these theories equally well save all *possible* evidence. So it seems one could be justified in believing an underdetermined theory. To this, we may add the point that subjects could reasonably disagree about the relative simplicity and explanatory power of competing theories, yet no further evidence would settle this disagreement. Moreover, subjects might reasonably differ in the relative *weights* they assign to simplicity and explanatory power in judging theories. From this, it follows that subjects might be justified in believing underdetermined competing theories. Since it seems that such underdetermination is left open by epistemology, and it ought not to be ruled impossible *by the nature of truth alone*, the superjustification theory must be rejected.

There is another way, besides underdetermination, in which superjustification might fail to be unique. Superjustification will fail to be unique if the observations on which theories are based are *theory-laden* in a certain way. If the observations a subject is justified in making depend for their justification on theories the subject holds, then it could happen that one subject is justified in one observation supporting one theory, and another is justified in a competing observation supporting a competing theory, even though both subjects possess as much relevant information as possible. No matter how much evidence is possessed, a proposition <*p*> constituting some observation may be superjustified and at the same time a contrary proposition <*q*> be superjustified. Admittedly, the claim that there are such theory-laden observations is far more controversial than the claim that there is underdetermination of the sort discussed above. Nevertheless, I do not think we want our theory of *truth* to rule out theory-laden observation. That honor should be arrogated to our epistemology.

The uniqueness objection highlights the fact that superjustification is relative to subjects in a way that truth is not. Of course, the proponent of the superjustification theory could parry the objection by relativizing truth to subjects, but only at the cost of inheriting the familiar troubles of relativism.

The superjustificationist might maintain, in the face of the objection, that there are surely certain topics for which truth coincides with superjustification. Plausibly, whether or not it is true that one is in pain is something for which there can be limited evidence beyond the justification one possesses, and the evidence will decide the matter one way or the other. Indeed, many have supposed that one is in pain just in case one is justified in believing that one is in pain—in which case, truth on this topic coincides, not merely with superjustification, but with justification. Equally plausibly, whether or not a joke is funny is something we can judge decisively with superjustification. Indeed, one might claim that these points follow from the meaning of "funny" and "pain."

I do not wish to contest these claims here. I will grant, at least for the sake of argument, that we can judge decisively with superjustification whether we are in pain or whether a joke is funny. But I do not see why we should hold that this has anything to do with the meaning of "true" or the nature of truth itself. If it has to do with the meaning of anything, it would have to do with the meaning of the language of humor and pain. The points here, in other words, hold because of the semantical features—the meanings—of propositions in specified domains, not because of features of truth in those domains. And so we are bereft of a case for the superjustification theory even on these limited topics.

Incompleteness Objection

Underdetermination may bear on the superjustification account in a slightly different way from the way in which it bears on the coherence theory. Suppose that there are examples of underdetermination in which competing theories are equally supported by all possible evidence and no theory is favored by theoretical desiderata. This may be true, for example, of the choice between general relativistic and neo-Newtonian theories of gravitation. It seems, then, that we should allow for the possibility of competing theories that are equally supported by all possible evidence, without any of the competing theories being theoretically preferable to the others. But where competing theories are equally supported by the evidence and none is favored by theoretical desiderata, it is plausible to deny that any theory is justified. (An empiricist will be committed to denying that any such theory is justified, but denying this has plausibility apart from empiricism.) In these circumstances, none of the competing theories will be superjustified. But then there will be true theories that are not superjustified. Since a theory of truth ought not by itself to decide the epistemological question whether there could be underdetermination of this sort, we must reject the superjustification theory.

Regress Objection

There is a further objection to the superjustification theory, one that tells against the coherence theory of truth as well. The theory gives rise to a regress parallel to the regress to which relativism and pragmatism give rise (see Chapter 2, Section III, and Chapter 3, Section III). As the issues here are essentially those we discussed earlier, we need not retrace them at this juncture. It suffices to say that the regress objection is just as compelling against the superjustification and other epistemic theories as against relativism and pragmatism.

Epistemological Objection

The superjustification theory and the coherence theory of truth misgauge our knowledge of truth in a manner analogous to the way in which pragmatism does (Chapter 3, Section III). Let me focus on the superjustification theory—similar points apply to the coherence theory.

One epistemological problem with the superjustification theory is that in general it makes knowing that a given proposition is true a more difficult achievement than it in fact is. It seems that I can be justified in believing *p* and be justified in believing that <*p*> is true, without at the same time being justified in believing that <*p*> is superjustified. To be justified in believing that *p* is superjustified, I must be justified in believing that: <*p*> is justified by some amount of evidence and no matter what further evidence concerning <*p*> may be acquired, <*p*> will remain justified. It is plausible enough that when I am justified in believing *p*, I am justified in believing that: as long as I acquire no further relevant evidence, I will remain justified in believing *p*. But it hardly follows from this that I am justified in believing that: there is some amount of evidence for <*p*> such that, if I possess this evidence and if I acquire relevant evidence, I will remain justified in believing *p*. And that is what is needed for me to be justified in believing that <*p*> is superjustified. I must be justified in believing that there are circumstances such that no further contrary evidence is sufficient to overturn my justification for believing *p*. And it is surely implausible that I can, for every superjustified <*p*> that I am justified in believing, be justified in such a strong claim about further evidence. On the contrary, I have inductive evidence that for many propositions I am justified in believing, there is no amount of evidence such that no further evidence will defeat my justification. And I have good reason to believe that superjustified propositions will be among these defeated propositions.

Now, the superjustificationist might reply that if I am justified in believing *p*, then I can become justified in believing what I can justifiedly infer from *p*. But one thing I can justifiedly infer is that <*p*> is superjustified. For if *p*, then, probably, there is an amount of evidence that justifies <*p*> such that no further evidence will trump the justification for believing *p*. So if I am justified in believing *p*, then I am justified in believing that I am superjustified in believing *p*.

As plausible as this reply may at first seem, it is ultimately unconvincing. First, the inference from <*p*> to the superjustification of <*p*> is justified only if there is no contrary evidence sufficient to defeat this justification. Yet the inductive evidence that, for many propositions I am justified in believing, there is no amount of evidence such that no further evidence will overturn my justification, is precisely a defeater of the justification for the inference. Second, underdetermination tells against the justification for the inference: there are true underdetermined theories that are not superjustified, so we ought not to infer from <*p*> to the superjustification of <*p*>. Thus, the reply to the epistemological objection fails and the objection stands.

The Point of the Notion of Truth

There is a final, somewhat elusive, but nevertheless potent objection to the superjustification and coherence theories. The theories make a mystery of the point of talk about truth. It seems clear that the notion of truth plays a significant role in human thought. Pragmatism is one theory of truth on which the notion of truth has a valuable intellectual role to play. The notion is valuable, on pragmatism, because assessing the truth of a proposition is nothing other than assessing the utility of believing it, and it is useful to make such assessments. Deflationism and the correspondence theory are also theories of truth that make the notion of truth valuable, as we will see in Chapters 5 and 6. The superjustification and coherence theories, in contrast, offer no comparable account of the value of the notion of truth. Indeed, they make it hard to grasp how the notion of truth could be valuable.

To see this, consider what use the notion of superjustification might have. The superjustification theory asks us, in judging whether propositions are true, to discern whether there is an amount of evidence for <*p*> such that no further evidence will defeat the justification for <*p*>. Yet it is far from clear why we should take an interest in that matter. Why would it be useful to judge whether a proposition is superjustified? Perhaps we should take an interest in the future course of evidence within the bounds of an inquiry we are conducting and perhaps, more distantly, we should take an interest in the course of evidence in the foreseeable future. These matters, after all, affect our current and future justification. But why should we take an interest in what would happen to the evidence in any possible course of inquiry? This is not a matter that affects our current or future justification.

To be sure, the availability of counterevidence in such further inquiry bears on whether the proposition is true. If we had any reason to think that sufficient counterevidence to overturn justification would be available in some further inquiry, we would have reason to doubt the proposition. But it is hard to see how we could have any such reason that would not also be a reason to think that such counterevidence *will* be available in the foreseeable future. Consequently, it is hard to see how we could have any use for the notion of superjustification that would not be served equally well by the notion of sufficient counterevidence in the foreseeable future. I cannot see any reason we might wish to employ the notion of superjustification. Similar remarks apply to the notion of truth-coherence and other epistemic notions of truth.

Of course the superjustificationist and the coherentist are entitled, as is any theorist of truth, to explain the utility of true belief contingently (see Chapter 3). The question here, however, is not the utility of true *belief* but of the *notion of truth* itself. It seems that the superjustification and the coherence theories entail the uselessness of the notion of truth. In this regard the pragmatic theory of truth has an advantage over epistemic theories. Since the notion of truth *is* evidently a valuable notion, the epistemic theories leave much to be desired.

These are the problems that beset epistemic theories of truth. The uniqueness, incompleteness, and epistemological objections pose a significant threat to these theories. The regress and the point of the notion of truth objections are forceful. In my view, these objections are enough to repel us from epistemic theories. I will have a bit more criticism of epistemic theories in Chapter 7. But our review of the historically important theories of truth has taken us far enough to conclude that the prospects for a theory of truth on which truth involves a dependency or other deep relation to thinkers—whether a relativist, pragmatist, or epistemic theory—are dim. The regress objection to these views, in particular, seems to generalize and leave only deflationism and the correspondence theory standing, at least among descriptive theories of truth (i.e., theories that define truth in descriptive language). It remains to ask, however, whether truth may nevertheless involve a relation to a truth-ascriber. That will turn out to be the key point at issue between the correspondence theory and deflationism, theories that will absorb our attention for the next two chapters.

Chapter Five

Deflationism

I. Deflationism

Having rejected the pragmatic and coherence theories of truth, we may turn to a more inviting theory, deflationism. The view is recent, by the ageless standards of the theory of truth. It was suggested, and at once dismissed, by the founder of twentieth-century philosophy of logic and language, Gottlob Frege (1960). Frank Ramsey (1927) is often credited with an early deflationary theory (but see Field 1986, 59-60, for doubts about Ramsey's commitment to deflationism). The theory has in fact received a nod of approval from a surprising plurality of the most distinguished philosophers of language and logic in this century—A. J. Ayer (1936), P. F. Strawson (1950), Ludwig Wittgenstein (1958), and W. V. Quine (1970). If it were possible to judge the correctness of an account of truth from the prominence of its recent adherents, deflationism might carry the day.

One virtue of deflationism is its simplicity, which derives, as does its very name, from its deflation of the pretensions assigned the concept of truth by the traditional theories of truth. The correspondence theory, pragmatism, and coherentism make truth a lofty matter. Deflationism makes it a trivial one. For the correspondentist, truth is a relation between a proposition, on the one hand, and a fact, state of affairs, or object and its properties, on the other. The pragmatist makes truth a matter of whether a proposition is useful to believe. Truth, for the coherentist, turns on how the proposition fits into a set of propositions or beliefs. The deflationist, on the other hand, denies that truth is any kind of relation to the world, and that truth is usefulness or coherence with beliefs. He or she proposes instead that the notion of truth in a given language is completely captured by the trivial truth-conditions or "T-sentences":

<*p*> is true just in case *p*

for each proposition <*p*> expressible in the language. That is, there is nothing more to truth than what is given by the truth-condition that *p*. This turns out, however, to make truth implicitly a relation to a truth-ascriber—a point of contention between deflationism and other theories of truth, and one that will matter greatly in deciding between deflationism and the correspondence theory.

This deflationary proposal is typically motivated by the view that there is nothing more to the nature of truth than a certain linguistic function of "true." The function of "true" in "<*p*> is true" is to make the assertion that would otherwise have to be made by uttering some other sentence expressing <*p*>. "True" enables the speaker to make such an assertion without actually employing or even knowing any sentence that expresses <*p*>. To ascribe truth to a proposition (or sentence) is not to attribute any property to the proposition (or sentence). It is rather to make an assertion that would be made using a sentence that expresses the proposition. "True" is, in effect, a logical operator on sentences on a par with logical connectives like "and" and "or." Just as there is nothing more to the nature of conjunction than a certain linguistic function of "and" characterized by the truth-table for "and" (where the truth-table for "and" says: <*p* and *q*> is true just in case <*p*> is true and <*q*> is true), so the notion of truth is completely captured by the trivial truth-conditions expressed by the T-sentences. The truth-condition ascribed to <*p*> or to a sentence expressing <*p*> using "true" is simply that *p*.

There are numerous ingenious versions of deflationism, but for our purposes it will be convenient to rely on the simple and elegant version proposed by Paul Horwich (1990). This version develops in a straightforward and powerful way the central idea of deflationism presented in the preceding paragraph (but see Wright 1992, 21n15, for one qualification of this). For ease of reference, I will call Horwich's version *T-sentence deflationism*. According to this version of deflationism, there is nothing more to truth than what is codified by the T-sentences of a language. I believe this view is as defensible as deflationism gets, but I will not be able to argue the point here.

Limitations of space prevent exploring differences between the various versions of deflationism, but to facilitate further discussion it would be desirable to mention one other version of deflationism before we proceed: *disquotational deflationism* (Quine 1970). On this version of deflationism, "true" performs the linguistic function, in effect, of removing the quotes from the names of sentences—i.e., the function of taking the name of a sentence (formed with quotes) and converting it into something that has the force of the sentence itself:

"‘*p*’ is true" means "*p*."

It is worth noting that, so formulated, disquotational deflationism is incomplete because it tells us only how "true" functions in sentences in which the grammatical subject is the name of a sentence formed with quotation marks around the sentence. There are, however, other ways of using "true"—as, e.g., in "What Elmo said is true" and "It is true that beavers have flat tails." But we need not complete the description of disquotational deflationism. (See Grover, Camp, and Belnap 1975, and C. J. F. Williams 1976 for other versions of deflationism and Kirkham 1992, 329-350, for an excellent review of the various versions.)

On T-sentence deflationism, there is nothing more to truth than what is captured by the T-sentences:

> $<p>$ is true just in case *p*.

So understood, T-sentence deflationism still leaves open a choice between two formulations. The theory might be formulated as *the list of T-sentences* (which, in the case of English, is infinite, since there is one T-sentence for each sentence of English, and there are infinitely many English sentences). Alternatively, the theory might be formulated as a *single* quantified sentence:

> For each proposition $<p>$, $<p>$ is true just in case *p*

where the quantifier "for each proposition $<p>$" is interpreted substitutionally. (I will explain momentarily what substitutional quantification is.)

On T-sentence deflationism, as on other versions of deflationism, the notion of truth is the notion of truth-in-a-language. That is, there is a different notion of truth for each language (or rather for each language that has the resources to express the concept of truth). This is because truth is defined by T-sentences, but there is a different set of T-sentences for each language. The notion of truth-in-a-language-*L* is defined by the T-sentences of *L*. T-sentence deflationism, then, entails that there is no one notion of truth. Rather, there are as many notions of truth as there are languages. Let it be noted, moreover, that the deflationary notion of truth-in-a-language-*L* is definable only in *L* (or in a language that contains *L* as a part). Thus, the only language in which truth-in-*L* could be defined for each language *L* is a language including all other languages. And of course there is no such all-inclusive language. So there is no language in which truth-in-*L* could be defined for each language *L*. To be sure, one might artificially expand the notion of truth-in-*L* to a notion of truth-in-$L+L'+L''+$ . . . by adding the T-sentences of various languages together. But this could be done only in a language containing all these T-sentences. And there is no such universal language.

All this marks a disturbing limitation of deflationism. Deflationism makes the notion of truth language-relative. On deflationism, the notion of truth is a notion of truth-in-*L*, and this notion is definable only in a metalanguage containing *L*. Yet the notion of truth does not seem to be language-relative at all. It does not seem to be a notion of truth-in-*L*. And it does not seem that the notion of truth applicable to sentences of *L* should be definable only in a metalanguage containing *L*.

There are ways for the deflationist to modify the view so as to avoid language relativity. The deflationist might amend the view so that an amended deflationary notion of truth-in-*L* can be defined in a language L' not containing *L* as a part. In particular, one may define truth-in-*L* in L' if L' has the expressive power of *L*—i.e., if for each sentence *S* of *L*, there is some sentence S' of L' that means the same thing as or expresses the same proposition as *S*, and there is in L' some way of expressing these meaning equivalences (something like the English "*S* in *L* means the same as S' in L'"). One may then define truth-in-*L* in L' in this way: add to the T-sentences of L' the sentences expressing these meaning equivalences. From all these sentences together, it is possible to deduce an analogue in L' of the T-sentences of *L*: *S* in *L* means the same as S' in L' and *S* is true just in case *p* (where "*p*" is the sentence referred to by "S'"). Thus, we will be able to define truth-in-French in English if English contains meaning equivalences for all French sentences. Truth-in-French is defined in English for "La neige est blanche" because English contains a sentence, "Snow is white," that means the same as "La neige est blanche" and can express this meaning equivalence, and English also contains a T-sentence for "Snow is white." We may (following Field 1986, 61) call the sort of deflationism here an *extended* deflationary definition of truth-in-*L* in *L*′.

Of course, it is intuitively implausible that English, or for that matter any other natural language, has the resources to express the propositions expressed by every sentence of every other natural language (or perhaps *any* other natural language). Thus, not even extended deflationism offers a way of capturing the notion of truth-in-*L* in English for every language *L*. So even on extended deflationism, there is no language in which all notions of truth can be defined. The proposed way of transcending the limitations of deflationism takes us only so far—and not as far as needed for intuitive plausibility.

As I mentioned, one impetus for T-sentence deflationism, as for other versions, is the claim that the linguistic function of "true" is simply to serve as a device for assenting to propositions expressed by sentences too numerous, lengthy, or cumbersome to utter or as a device for assenting to propositions when it is unknown which sentences express the propositions. (By the *linguistic function* of "true" here I mean something like the contribution of this predicate to what one asserts in uttering sentences in which the predicate appears.) One says "Euclidean geometry is true" in lieu of uttering sentences that express the axioms of Euclidean geometry. Of course, in the case of infinite sets of propositions, there must be some finite way to *specify* the propositions that belong to the set (e.g., in elementary arithmetic the principle of mathematical induction consists of infinitely many axioms, but these fall under a single axiom schema). In this way, one can assent to an infinite set of propositions by uttering the schema without using "true." However, one cannot *dissent* from an infinite set of propositions without using "true" if one cannot say from which propositions of the theory one dissents. For there is no finite conjunction of propositions of the theory from which one dissents. So one needs "true" to dissent from an infinite set of propositions.

Now, one could assent to and dissent from these propositions without using "true" by uttering "I assent to Euclidean geometry" and the like. This would effect assent. However, the sentence employed in effecting assent here does not entail that Euclidean geometry is true, so one cannot in this way express what one would express by uttering each sentence of Euclidean geometry. It is worth noting that one cannot employ even this means to effect assent in one's *beliefs*, as opposed to utterances. When one wants to believe what another says, but one does not know just which propositions the other believes, one must employ the concept of truth. If one wants to assent in belief to whatever Einstein says, one cannot merely believe that one assents to whatever Einstein says. That would merely entail a belief about what one assents to; it would not entail assent to the propositions expressed by Einstein. To effect belief in those propositions, one needs to believe that whatever Einstein says is true.

Another way to put these points is to say that "true" is equivalent, according to the deflationist, to a device of *infinite conjunction* or of *substitutional quantification*. The device of infinite conjunction enables one to conjoin infinitely many sentences in a single sentence:

p_1 and p_2 and . . .

We may write this as:

$\text{Conjunction}_{i=1,\ldots}(p_i)$.

Thus

Conjunction (*p*: Einstein accepts that *p*)

(read: "the conjunction of sentences '*p*' such that Einstein accepts that *p*") is a conjunction of all sentences Einstein accepts. Of course there are no infinite conjunctions in English. English sentences are finite in length. "True," however, gives the effect of infinite conjunction by enabling us to assent simultaneously to all propositions in an infinite set of propositions to which truth is ascribed. Thus, "Anything Einstein accepts is true" is equivalent to "Conjunction (*p*: Einstein accepts that *p*)."

The device of substitutional quantification may also be used to effect assent to infinitely many sentences. Since substitutional quantification will play a significant role in our discussion of deflationism and the correspondence theory, it is worth getting clear about what it is. Substitutional quantification contrasts with *objectual* quantification. In quantification of the latter kind, the variable "*x*" governed by a quantifier such as "for all objects *x*" ranges over objects in an assumed domain. Thus, "For all objects *x*, *x* is a zebra" means that each object in an assumed domain is a zebra. In substitutional quantification, in contrast, the variable "*x*" does not range over objects. "For all *x*, *x* is a zebra" stands in place of the set of sentences of the form "*a* is a zebra," for each name "*a*" in an assumed language. This is an example of substitutional quantification employing a variable that stands in place of *names*. There is also substitutional quantification employing a variable that stands in place of *sentences*. And that kind of substitutional quantification enables one to get the effect of infinite conjunction. Instead of saying "Anything Einstein accepts is true," you quantify substitutionally, saying

For any $<p>$, (if Einstein accepts that *p*, then *p*).

T-sentence deflationism explains how "true" can perform the linguistic function of assent. The T-sentences in effect eliminate "true" from all sentences in which "true" is predicated of a term referring to a sentence. This elimination explains how a sentence in which "true" is predicated of such a term can stand in place of a sentence to which the term refers. In short, for propositions expressed by sentences, we can account for truth by the infinite list of T-sentences. The T-sentences *directly* eliminate "true" from all sentences in which "true" is predicated of the quotational nominalization of some sentence (that is, predicated of the name of a sentence formed by putting the sentence in quotes). And the T-sentences *indirectly* define "true" for sentences that predicate truth of sentences without naming the latter by quotational nominalization. For example, "true" in "What he said is true" is indirectly defined by the T-sentence for the sentence referred to by "what he said." In this way, the T-sentences explain the assent function of "true."

In favor of deflationism, it must be said that "true" certainly does perform the linguistic function the deflationist claims for it: "true" does have an assent function. And any plausible theory of truth will have to explain how "true" manages to perform this function. Since deflationism explains how "true" does the trick, it has a significant merit. I agree with the deflationist that *if* "true" performed *only* the linguistic function of assent, *and if* the nature of truth were *entirely* captured by the linguistic function of "true," then deflationism would prevail. But neither of these assumptions is secure.

II. Objections to Deflationism

To see that there is more to truth than the deflationist allows, we need only observe that deflationism assigns mistaken truth-conditions to propositions. For the T-sentences are incomplete, and many of them are in fact false. Thus they do not give the truth-conditions for all propositions. Let us examine this charge in some detail.

Counterfactual Objection

The objection I have in mind here is easiest to see for a disquotational version of deflationism—the view that "*p*" is true just in case *p*—and I will begin with the version of the objection that applies to disquotational deflationism. On this kind of deflationism, certain counterfactual conditional sentences turn out to be equivalent even though intuition strongly tells us that they are not. Thus, disquotational deflationism runs afoul of strong intuitions and must be rejected.

Recall, from our discussion in Chapter 1, that a counterfactual conditional sentence is a sentence of the form "If it were the case that *p*, then it would be the case that *q*." Such a conditional is called "counterfactual" because the antecedent of the conditional—the part of the sentence between "if" and "then"—is contrary to fact. The counterfactual objection to disquotational deflationism, then, is that the view makes intuitively nonequivalent counterfactual conditional sentences equivalent and thus gets the truth-conditions of these counterfactual conditional sentences wrong. Indeed, it even gets the *truth-values* of these sentences wrong.

To see the objection, consider this pair of counterfactual conditional sentences:

> If we had used "snow" differently (e.g., to mean grass), "Snow is white" would not have been true.
>
> If we had used "snow" differently (e.g., to mean grass), snow would not have been white.

These sentences are *equivalent* on disquotational deflationism because "'Snow is white' is true" is equivalent to "Snow is white." But these sentences are clearly not equivalent in any *ordinary* sense of "true." On the contrary, the first is true and the second false. Whether or not snow is white would not be at all affected by how we use "snow," whereas whether "Snow is white" is true would be very much affected. This seems to show that truth in application to sentences is a relation between words and the world, as the correspondence theorist claims it is, and not something wholly captured by facts about the world. But then disquotational deflationism is mistaken, since it implies that truth is wholly captured by facts about the world. These and other examples point rather obstinately in the direction of a correspondence theory of truth: truth is a relation between words and the world.

Now, so far we have an objection only to disquotational deflationism. It is trickier to formulate an objection of this sort to *T-sentence* deflationism, since the latter takes propositions rather than sentences as the bearers of truth-values. Nevertheless, an objection can be formulated. The formulation requires that we assume that just as truth is defined by the T-sentences, so falsehood is defined by the F-sentences:

<*p*> is false just in case not-*p*

for each proposition <*p*> expressible in the language. This is a natural and perhaps inescapable assumption for a deflationist. In any event, the deflationist would appear to have no other resources for characterizing falsehood.

Once we assume the F-sentences, we may pose the objection to T-sentence deflationism this way. Consider this pair of counterfactual conditional sentences:

> If we had no sentence to express either <Snow is white> or <Snow is not white>, then it would not be the case that <Snow is white> is true, and it would not be the case that <Snow is white> is false.

> If we had no sentence to express either <Snow is white> or <Snow is not white>, then it would not be the case that snow is white, and it would not be the case that snow is not white.

On T-sentence deflationism the first of these counterfactual sentences is true. But the two sentences are equivalent on T-sentence deflationism. Yet intuitively the second sentence is false: it would still be the case that snow is white or that snow is not white, even if we had no sentence to express either <Snow is white> or <Snow is not white>. Thus, T-sentence deflationism runs afoul of our intuitions about the truth-conditions of certain counterfactual conditional sentences.[1]

As far as I can see, the T-sentence deflationist can reply to this counterfactual objection only by relinquishing a claim to capture the sense of "true" employed in these counterfactual conditional sentences. The T-sentence deflationist might deny that "<*p*> is true" can be substituted for "*p*" in the consequents of counterfactual conditional sentences, as the objection requires. But this denial carries a price: it would require relinquishing the claim that "<*p*> is true" is equivalent to "*p*" in a manner permitting such a substitution. Perhaps T-sentence deflationism is not intended to claim an equivalence that supports substitutions like these. The deflationist may intend only the much weaker claim that "<*p*> is true" is *extensionally* equivalent to—has the same truth value as—"*p*." But if so, then deflationism falls short of explaining the behavior of "true" in modal contexts—something to which other theories of truth aspire.

Alternatively, the T-sentence deflationist may reply to the counterfactual objection by admitting that deflationism does not characterize every ordinary use of "true." The deflationist will wish to insist, however, that a notion of truth of the sort characterized by deflationism is needed. For we need *some* predicate that can perform the linguistic function assigned "true" by deflationism. We need to be able to assent to and dissent from propositions expressed by sentences unknown or too numerous, lengthy, or cumbersome to utter.

Whether this reply to the counterfactual objection is adequate depends on whether we must introduce a new predicate "true" characterized by T-sentence deflationism in order to handle the linguistic function the deflationist assigns "true." I agree that we need a predicate to perform this function. But I also believe that the ordinary predicate "true" can perform it. And I see no reason to suppose that deflationism must characterize the predicate that performs the function. To be sure, when the predicate "true" performs the function, it must obey the relevant T-sentences. But it does not follow that the T-sentences must hold for propositions to which "true" can be applied. Nor does it follow that the T-sentences must exhaust the meaning of "true" in the cases in which "true" is used to perform the function, as the deflationist claims.

It might be charged that "true" as characterized by nondeflationary theories of truth, e.g., the correspondence theory, cannot perform the required linguistic function. To be sure, on the correspondence theory, in uttering "Anything Einstein says is true," we succeed only in saying that the propositions expressed by Einstein's utterances correspond to the world. But equally, on the correspondence theory, "<*p*> is true" entails <*p*> for any proposition <*p*> to which we should wish to assent. (There are exceptions to this entailment in, for example, borderline cases of vagueness, but in these cases, we should not wish to assent to <*p*>.) So, in uttering "Anything Einstein says is true," we are committed to the propositions Einstein utters. Admittedly, this falls short of using "true" to assent *only* to what Einstein assented to in his utterances, since we assent as well to propositions about correspondences. Nevertheless, in using "true," we do *assent* to the propositions

Einstein expressed in his utterances. Plausibly, on the correspondence theory, "true" can be used for the function that deflationism assigns it. So, in the end, the fact that "true" performs this function cannot be used to support deflationism.

Bivalence Objection

Let us turn now to a second objection to deflationism. According to this objection, deflationary truth-conditions are incorrect, since deflationism entails *Bivalence*, the principle that every proposition is either true or false. But that principle is mistaken.

Why does deflationism entail Bivalence? On deflationism, for every proposition <*p*>, <*p*> is true just in case *p*. Suppose, however, that Bivalence does not hold—i.e., for some proposition <*p*>, <*p*> is neither true nor false. Then the right-hand side of the T-sentence for <*p*>, "*p*," has *no truth value*, but the left-hand side, "<*p*> is true," has the value *false*, since it is false that <*p*> is true (because <*p*> has no truth-value). So the T-sentence fails. Consequently, if Bivalence fails, so does deflationism. But by the principle of Contraposition (i.e., the principle that "if *p*, then *q*" is equivalent to "if not-*q*, then not-*p*"), this is the same as saying that deflationism entails Bivalence.

Now the objection to deflationism is that Bivalence is mistaken. For this principle succumbs to counterexamples, the most secure being borderline cases of vagueness. If Joe has a borderline case of baldness, then <Joe is bald> is neither true nor false, even though it may still be the case that either Joe is bald or he is not bald. Vagueness entails that Bivalence fails. But then, since deflationism entails Bivalence, deflationism also fails.

There are three possible replies to the Bivalence objection:

(1) The deflationist may reply that for vague propositions <*p*>, "*p*" and "<*p*> is true" have the same truth-value—are true, false, or of indeterminate truth-value together. In this case, one may reject Bivalence without having to relinquish the T-sentences (Wright 1992, 61-62). The trouble with this reply is that it is hard to see how "*p*" could have indeterminate truth-value while "<*p*> is true" also has indeterminate truth-value. If "*p*" has indeterminate truth-value, then it is not merely not true but downright false that <*p*> has the value true. So "<*p*> is true" is false.

(2) The deflationist may reply in a different way—by denying that vagueness is a counterexample to Bivalence (Field 1986, 68-70, Horwich 1990, 80-87). According to this reply, vague sentences are either true or false. This reply can carry conviction, however, only if the deflationist finds a way to recognize that in *some* sense vague sentences in borderline cases are not *fully* true or false. The challenge for this response is to say in what sense borderline vague sentences fall short of full truth and falsity.

The deflationist who gives this reply may put a label on the sense in which borderline vague sentences fall short of full truth and falsity: vague sentences are neither *definitely true* nor *definitely false* (though, according to the present reply, they are still either true or false—we can't say which). One way to understand definite truth and falsity is to introduce a "definitely" qualifier in terms of which these notions are defined. The "definitely" qualifier is to be related to "definitely true" and "definitely false" in such a manner that if Joe has a borderline case of baldness, then he is not definitely bald nor is he definitely not bald. The deflationist defines "definitely true" in terms of the "definitely" qualifier by the DT-sentences:

<*p*> is definitely true just in case definitely *p*

for each proposition <*p*> expressible in the language. Similarly, "definitely false" is defined by the DF-sentences:

<*p*> is definitely false just in case definitely not-*p*

for each proposition <*p*> expressible in the language. For example, "Joe is bald" is neither definitely true nor definitely false, since Joe is not definitely bald nor is he definitely not bald. Nevertheless, it remains the case that <Joe is bald> is either true or false. Bivalence is preserved while recognizing that borderline vague sentences fall short of full truth and falsity.

Now, this reply to the Bivalence objection can be satisfying only if the deflationist can offer some grasp of the "definitely" qualifier. The trouble is that it is unclear what account of the qualifier can be given. Some account is required if the deflationist is to get us to admit that we ought to say, not that borderline vague propositions are neither true nor false, but that they are neither definitely true nor definitely false. But what account can be given? Clearly any account will have to appeal to resources beyond what the deflationist offers as an account of "true."

There is, however, an alternative to explicating "definitely true" and "definitely false" in terms of the "definitely" qualifier. One may make "definitely true" an *epistemological* notion (Field 1986, 68-70, Horwich 1990, 80-87):

<Joe is bald> is definitely true just in case we can have good reason to believe that Joe is bald.

On this way of recognizing that borderline vague sentences fall short of full truth and falsity, the commonsense claim that <Joe is bald> is neither true nor false is merely a badly muddled and highly misleading rendering of the epistemological view that we cannot have good reason to believe that Joe is bald or that Joe is not bald. But it is hard to accept that we are so befuddled. When we say that <Joe is bald> is neither true nor false, we do not merely think that we lack reason to believe that Joe is bald. Indeed, it seems that we could have all the evidence that might be relevant to whether Joe is bald—e.g., we could know the exact number of hairs on Joe's head—and yet we would *still* think that <Joe is bald> has indeterminate truth-value. We evidently think that there is something about nature itself that prevents <Joe is bald> from being true or false. It is not merely that we are ignorant here, but that there is nothing to know: nothing we could know, were we to learn everything nature would have to tell us, would decide the truth-value of <Joe is bald>. Our claim is a semantical-metaphysical one, not an epistemological one. Of course, the deflationist might protest that even if we knew the number of hairs on Joe's head, we would still lack one crucial piece of information relevant to whether Joe is bald: the exact number of hairs it takes to count as bald. But this is at best a counter-intuitive proposal. There does not seem to be any exact number of hairs it takes to be bald. For this reason, the epistemological account of "definitely true" is inadequate. It is unclear whether the deflationist has any satisfactory account of "definitely true" to offer.

(3) There is one last defense of deflationism from the objection that it entails Bivalence and is thus mistaken. This defense, unlike (1) and (2), dispenses with Bivalence. It allows that Bivalence is mistaken and is so because of borderline vagueness. It denies, however, that deflationism entails Bivalence. Bivalence follows from deflationism only on the assumption that deflationism entails a T-sentence for every sentence "*p*" in the language, including sentences describing states of affairs with borderline vagueness. But, so goes the defense, deflationism need only entail the T-sentences for sentences that do not describe cases of borderline vagueness.

Now, one might wonder what then happens to the deflationist idea that truth is characterized by the T-sentences. The answer is that the deflationist need embrace only those T-sentences that are required to explain the linguistic function of "true." In a borderline case of baldness, it could happen that Joe is bald but <Joe is bald> is not true. In this case, the T-sentence

<Joe is bald> is true just in case Joe is bald

is not true, since the right-hand side holds but the left-hand side is false. But, according to the present line of reasoning, the failure of this T-sentence should not worry the deflationist. For in this case, we would not use "true" to perform the linguistic function of enabling us to assent to the proposition <Joe is bald>. We would not assent to that proposition, since we do not know whether Joe is bald or Joe is not bald. We do not take sides in a borderline case of vagueness. So we have no need to use "true" to assent to the proposition. In general, the deflationist need only embrace the T-sentences for vague sentences in cases that are not borderline, since only in those cases do we use "true" to assent to a proposition.

Unfortunately, this defense is open to an unsettling reply. Suppose the deflationist tries to embrace some T-sentences and not others. Then the question arises why some T-sentences hold and others do not. The trouble is that the deflationist has no way to answer this question. When asked to say why, on deflationism, the T-sentences in borderline cases of vagueness do not hold, the deflationist can only say that if they did hold, then there would be counterexamples to deflationism. But of course this is an ad hoc answer. The deflationist has no way to explain why certain T-sentences hold and others do not. What needs to be explained is why in borderline cases of vagueness, *p* but <*p*> is not true. And deflationism is congenitally incapable of explaining this. For the deflationist simply *defines* truth by certain T-sentences—defines it in such a way that in borderline cases of vagueness, the T-sentences do not hold. The deflationist's concept of truth is too impoverished to offer any explanation here. It seems the explanation ought to appeal to the way the world is—indeterminate in borderline cases of vagueness—and to the nature of truth—indeterminate when the world is indeterminate. But this explication requires a theory of truth on which truth mirrors reality in a certain way. That is, it requires a *correspondence theory of truth*. Thus, the deflationist cannot adequately respond to the vagueness objection merely by rejecting the T-sentences in cases of borderline vagueness.

In short, borderline vagueness is a powerful, if not overwhelming, obstacle to the acceptance of a deflationary theory of truth. It seems that to account for the truth-conditions of vague sentences, we require the services of a correspondence theory of truth.

Incompleteness Objection

A third and final objection to deflationism is that the T-sentences are too shallow to specify the truth-conditions for all propositions. We can see this by observing that they do not provide a complete account of the linguistic function of "true." The predicate "true" appears in many sentences in which its linguistic function cannot be explained by appeal to the T-sentences.

Look, for example, at the sentence "What God believes is true." There are not enough T-sentences in English to define "true" in such a way as to cover this sentence. For presumably God believes many propositions not expressible in English, and the truth-conditions of these propositions are not covered by the T-sentences. The problem here arises because deflationism makes truth implicitly a relation to the truth-ascriber.

I would add that it is intuitively highly implausible that "What God believes" would be used merely (if at all) as a way of assenting to the propositions God believes (though uttering this sentence nevertheless commits one to those propositions). Moreover, the meaning of "true" in this sentence does not seem markedly different from its meaning in sentences like "Anything Einstein believes is true." Yet if this is so, then the latter sentence is not used merely to assent to what Einstein believes. This raises the possibility, in line with my earlier remarks on how the correspondence theory could explain the linguistic function of "true," that the assent function of "true" is incidental to its meaning, belonging to the *pragmatics* rather than the *semantics* of "true." That is, the assent function does not derive from and is not represented in the meaning of "true."

The deflationist might reply to this objection in either of two ways. One way is to insist that English must be capable of expressing all propositions. This way of replying must surely be a last, heroic resort. Even if we grant current English such expressive powers, we must balk at the idea that every language with a truth predicate is so expressive. The English language of thirty years ago had fewer powers to express notions about computers than current English. The deflationist could, I suppose, insist that English thirty years ago had the expressive power to define the new notions about computers now expressible in English. But this proposal falls into the realm of the preposterous as we slip back to the language of Chaucer.

A second heroic reply to the objection is to insist that we only use "true" to assent to sentences that can be translated into English. This would perhaps allow us to say "Anything Einstein says is true." But it would prevent us from assenting to what God believes and from saying, "What God believes is true." This is a heroic measure because in applying "true" to propositions we do not in practice observe any such restriction. Our willingness to apply "true" to a proposition does not vary at all with our power to express the proposition in English, as it should if "true" were deflationary.

The deflationist might respond that English speakers, in using "true," simply assume without thinking that the propositions to which it is applied are expressible in English. But if this were so, then our willingness to apply "true" should be diminished by doubts about the expressibility of a proposition in English. And it is not. Alternatively, the deflationist might allege that English speakers, even the most philosophically sophisticated of them, habitually use "true" in a manner inconsistent with its meaning. But surely the habitual use of a term is (in a broad sense of "use" to include reference, and with exceptions for meaning indebted to expert use) constitutive of its meaning. In this regard, note that even philosophically sophisticated speakers do not lose their willingness to ascribe "true" when apprised that a proposition is inexpressible in English. Thus, I am inclined to persist in thinking that the present incompleteness objection to deflationism is a serious one. It is worth noting here that the incompleteness objection turns, as did the counterfactual objection, on the fact that deflationism counterintuitively makes truth implicitly a relation to the truth-ascriber.

In this chapter, we have seen some advantages and disadvantages of deflationism.[2] The view does straightforwardly explain one important linguistic function of "true"—to assent to propositions. But it is by no means clear that this linguistic function should be represented in the semantics—the account of the meaning—of "true," rather than in the pragmatics of "true." Moreover, the correspondence theory is capable of explaining this linguistic function of "true." And in any event deflationism's advantage here is purchased at the cost of incorrect and incomplete truth-conditions. The case against deflationism thus seems to me weighty. Deflationism faces three serious objections: the counterfactual, Bivalence, and incompleteness objections. The Bivalence objection, in particular, suggests a move to the correspondence theory. It is time, therefore, to consider the plausibility of that theory.

Chapter Six

The Correspondence Theory

By now the reader will suspect my sympathies. I favor the correspondence theory of truth:

> A proposition is true just in case it corresponds to facts or the world.

The theory is usually traced to Plato's *Theaetetus* and *Sophist* (1973a, 1973b) and is customarily attributed to Aristotle, the Stoics, numerous medieval philosophers, Descartes, Locke, Hume, Moore, and Russell, among others.

The correspondence theorist must explain what it is for a proposition to correspond to facts or the world. I believe it is best to let the account of correspondence emerge from the arguments for the correspondence theory. The key point of contention between the correspondence theory and deflationism is whether truth implicitly involves a relation to a truth-ascriber. The deflationist holds that it does, while the correspondence theorist denies this. By and large, the arguments for the correspondence theory turn on this matter, as did the counterfactual and incompleteness objections to deflationism.

Before going into the arguments for the correspondence theory, however, we had best take our bearings. The correspondence theory is not committed to any particular ontological position on the nature of facts or the world. Most correspondence theorists have been realists, but the view is consistent with an idealist as well as a realist ontology. Indeed, there are idealists who have been correspondence theorists. Immanuel Kant, despite the common attribution to him of a coherence theory of truth, may be a prominent example (Kant 1965, A58). Nor, as I will argue below, will a choice between realism and idealism affect the ability of the correspondence theory to do the jobs it is intended to do. Despite this independence of the correspondence theory from the realism-idealism issue, what is at stake between the correspondence theory and other theories of truth bears an important resemblance to what divides realism and idealism: whether truth is something that has to do with us. The fundamental advantage of the correspondence theory over other theories of truth parallels the fundamental advantage of realism over idealism: the correspondence theory allows us to avoid making truth something that has to do with us. The theory differs from relativism, pragmatism, and coherentism in denying that truth involves, by its nature or by virtue of the meaning of "true," a deep relation to believers. It differs from epistemic theories in denying that, by virtue of meaning or nature, truth depends on the mind. (For this reason, the theory rules out one sort of idealism, if epistemic theories are taken as expressing an idealism.) And it differs from deflationism in denying that truth involves a relation to a truth-ascriber. As I have already indicated, it is on this last point that the arguments for the correspondence theory will turn.

I. Arguments for the Correspondence Theory

Though from a long-range historical perspective, the correspondence theory is by far the most popular theory of truth, hardly anyone has ever bothered to argue for the view. Proponents of the theory have usually rested on its intuitive obviousness. But as several writers have recently observed, the intuitions that allegedly support the theory turn out, upon close inspection, to be nothing more than platitudes that can be accepted by deflationists. The theory thus stands in need of serious argument. It happens that we owe virtually all the notable arguments to one philosopher, Hartry Field (1972, 1986). These arguments undoubtedly owe some inspiration to Putnam's earlier work on realism, and they have been inventively developed by others (Devitt 1984, for example). But Field must receive credit for the articulation. I propose to defend these arguments and some others Field rejects (in particular, (1) below). What I add to Field's account is mainly accessibility.

To make a case for the correspondence theory, we may begin with the upshot of Chapters 3, 4, and 5: there is no plausible alternative theory of truth. Pragmatism and coherentism suffer from a variety of ills. These theories may well be committed to relativism, and in any case face serious regress and epistemological objections. The main source of their inadequacy is that they make truth depend on us in a way that it intuitively does not. Deflationism promised a way around this difficulty. Yet on further inspection we could see that it too succumbs to the difficulty. Deflationism mishandles certain counterfactual conditionals, rules out borderline vagueness in language, and entails that truth can be predicated only of propositions expressible in English. The first and third of these problems arise because on deflationism, truth implicitly involves a relation to a truth-ascriber. All three problems with deflationism suggest the correspondence theory by way of solution.

Rather than pursue these particular matters further, I will follow Field in arguing for the correspondence theory on the ground that a correspondence notion of truth is needed if truth-conditions are to play their role in explaining human behavior and in explaining as well certain successful practices. A deflationary notion of truth cannot serve in truth-conditions in the required capacity because it entails that truth implicitly involves a relation to a truth-ascriber.

Explaining Behavior

The first claim that might be made on behalf of the correspondence theory is that when we explain human behavior by ascribing beliefs and desires, we implicitly use a correspondence notion of truth. I will focus here on the explanation of bodily behavior, but similar points may be made about the explanation of cognitive behavior and inference (about which I will say more below).

Commonsense explanation of behavior adverts to the beliefs and desires of the subject. To explain why Skip performed the action of going to the grocer, we refer to Skip's desire that he acquire food and his belief that by going to the grocer he will acquire food. We would most naturally understand this as a causal explanation in which it is assumed that the belief and the desire together cause the action. But we need not decide here whether belief-desire explanation is causal explanation, since the question of causation does not enter into the argument for the correspondence theory.

The argument for the correspondence theory is this (Field 1986, 82-89). Ascribing beliefs and desires to others for purposes of explaining their behavior requires ascribing *propositional contents* to these beliefs and desires. That is, it requires treating the beliefs and desires as having propositions as contents. Thus, to explain Skip's trip to the grocer, I ascribe to him a desire that has the propositional content that he acquires food, and I also ascribe to him a belief that has the propositional content that by going to the grocer he will acquire food. These ascriptions of a belief and a desire involve at the same time ascriptions of specific propositional contents to the belief and the desire. But to ascribe contents to beliefs and desires is to ascribe *truth-conditions* to these beliefs and desires, since propositions necessarily carry with them truth-conditions. If I ascribe the content <By going to the grocer I will acquire food> to Skip's belief, then I ascribe to his belief the truth-conditions of this proposition. To ascribe a content to a belief is to treat it as being true or false. (Admittedly, to ascribe a content to a desire would not normally be understood as treating it as true or false. We do not normally speak of desires as true or false. Nevertheless, ascribing a content to a desire does ascribe truth-conditions to it. Desires also have *satisfaction-conditions*—conditions under which they are satisfied. The satisfaction-condition of a desire is, however, the condition under which the proposition ascribed to the desire is true.)

Once it is agreed that explaining behavior requires ascribing truth-conditions to beliefs and desires, the correspondentist proceeds by arguing that these truth-conditions must be *correspondence* truth-conditions. They cannot be deflationary truth-conditions (or pragmatic or coherence truth-conditions, either). For if the truth-conditions were deflationary (or pragmatic or coherentist), then we would in effect explain the behavior of others by relating their states to ourselves. This is because deflationism gives truth-conditions only for propositions *expressible in English*. The truth-conditions given by deflationism are essentially related to the language of those ascribing truth-conditions. Thus, if deflationary truth-conditions are ascribed in explaining behavior, the behavior is explained by relating it to the language of the explainers. But the explanation of a person's behavior ought to refer only to the relation between the person's beliefs, desires, and environment. It ought to have nothing to do with us as explainers of the person's behavior, or with our language. But once we have ruled out deflationary, pragmatic, coherence, and all other truth-conditions that relate the subject's behavior to the content-ascriber, the only truth-conditions that remain are correspondence truth-conditions. So we need a correspondence notion of truth to explain behavior. This is the explanatory argument for the correspondence theory.

It is worth pausing to consider whether this argument, with its insistence that the explanation of behavior and thus truth-conditions not relate the subject to us, the explainers, commits its proponent to realism. One might think so. For on idealism, the existence of objects and facts has to do with us. So, on idealism, it cannot be that the explanation of a person's behavior ought to refer only to the relation between the person's beliefs, desires, and environment; it must refer to us, the explainers of the person's behavior. The proponent of the explanatory argument must, it seems, reject idealism. In other words, the explanatory argument entails realism.

But despite these appearances, the argument does not really saddle the correspondence theorist with realism. True, it assumes that the explanation of behavior refers only to the relation between beliefs, desires, and the environment—and nothing else. The problem with deflationism is that it entails, incorrectly, that the explanation does not refer only to the relation between these items. And an idealist will understand these items as dependent on the mind. But this does not forbid the idealist from distinguishing between an explanation that refers only to a relation between beliefs, desires, and the environment and an explanation that refers to other things as well, such as the language of the explainer. For the idealist, this will of course be a distinction between kinds of explanations all of which refer to mind-dependent relations. But the nature of the mind-dependent relations to which the explanations refer will nevertheless differ for the idealist. The relation to which the explanation of behavior refers, according to the argument, will not itself be a relation to the language of the explainer, as it is on deflationism. This is so, despite the fact that for the idealist this relation, like everything else, depends on the mind.

To put the point differently, the argument from explaining behavior shows only that truth does not depend on us, *except* perhaps in so far as it is made to do so by the way the world is. Even if, as the idealist holds, objects depend on us, there is still a distinction between accounts of truth on which truth depends on us only because objects do, and an account of truth on which truth depends on us for some further reason (such as that truth involves an implicit relation to a truth-ascriber). Deflationism is a view of truth of the latter kind, the correspondence theory of the former kind. Since deflationism entails that the truth has to do with us for semantical and not ontological reasons—hence has to do with us regardless of whether it is made to do so by the way the world is—the argument from explaining behavior tells against deflationism. It does not, however, tell against idealism, since idealism entails only that the truth depends on us as a consequence of the way the world is. Thus, the argument from explaining behavior does not prevent one from combining the correspondence theory of truth with idealism. The correspondence theory and idealism are every bit as compatible as, superficially, they appear to be.

This said, what is at issue between the correspondence theorist and the deflationist does closely parallel what is at stake between the realist and the idealist. For it concerns whether in any way truth involves a relation to us—the deflationist holding that it does (at least at one remove) and the correspondence theorist denying this. The parallel here has its limits, however. For the points pro and con each side in the two issues differ importantly, owing both to their differing status as semantical and ontological issues and to the fact that the issue between the correspondence theory and deflationism specifically concerns whether truth involves a relation to the truth-ascriber, while the idealism-realism dispute does not turn on whether the existence of objects involves a relation to an existence-ascriber.

With the explanatory argument before us and preliminary matters out of the way, we may ask how persuasive the argument is. I see two vulnerable spots.

(1) The explanatory argument assumes that explaining behavior requires ascribing beliefs and desires (and thus propositional contents to beliefs and desires). This assumption might be denied on the ground that we can explain behavior *syntactically*—without ascribing beliefs, desires, and without ascribing propositional contents to beliefs and desires. That is, we can explain behavior by ascribing states with which we associate uninterpreted syntax (Stich 1983, 149-183).

A syntactical explanation of Skip's trip to the grocer would proceed in this way. I ascribe to Skip a cognitive state—call it a *B-state*—associated with the uninterpreted string of symbols "By going to the grocer I will acquire food." I also ascribe to him a motivational state—call it a *D-state*—associated with the uninterpreted string of symbols "I acquire food." I then explain Skip's behavior via a law relating B-states associated with certain syntax and D-states associated with related syntax to actions (in this case, going to the grocer). Simplifying enormously, the law would say:

> When a subject is in a B-state associated with the uninterpreted string of symbols "By going to the grocer I will acquire food" and a D-state associated with the uninterpreted string of symbols "I acquire food," then the subject tends to go to the grocer.

In explaining Skip's behavior by appeal to this law, I do not assign content to the B-states and D-states. Consequently, I do not ascribe truth-conditions at all. If we can explain all behavior in this syntactical way, we can explain behavior without ascribing beliefs and desires, propositional contents, and truth-conditions, and the argument from explaining behavior falls through.

One rejoinder to this syntactical reply to the argument is that even if we *need* not employ beliefs and desires to explain behavior, the fact remains that we do. And the argument still shows that people who explain behavior in a commonsense way are committed to the correspondence theory. Not only this, but even if a syntactical explanation of behavior is possible, it is doubtful that anyone knows the syntactically specified laws of psychology to which one would have to appeal to explain behavior syntactically. In other words, the syntactical explanation of behavior is unavailable, currently and for the foreseeable future. Belief-desire explanation appears to be the only form of explanation available to us. Of course the proponent of syntactical explanation might respond that no one knows the semantically specified psychological laws either. But it seems obvious that we do know enough to explain behavior by appeal to beliefs and desires, so if explaining behavior requires knowing laws, then we must know the laws. At the same time, the syntactically specified laws (assuming there really are any) differ to at least some extent from the semantically specified laws (Stich 1983, 149-183) and in ways that demand the sort of knowledge that can only be acquired by sophisticated observation and experiment. There is no ordinary form of explanation in which people engage that could require knowledge of the syntactically specified laws. The upshot is that we are at least practically speaking committed to a correspondence theory of truth.

Another rejoinder to the syntactical reply is that one cannot really explain behavior in a purely syntactical way. For an explanation of behavior via the law just mentioned is possible only if syntax is assigned to the B-states and D-states in such a way that not only this law comes out true but many other laws come out true as well. But such a systematic assignment of syntax will be parasitic on the assignment of contents to cognitive states. So contents must be assigned after all.

To see this, observe that the assignment of syntax—of the uninterpreted strings of symbols—to the beliefs and desires in this case and to other similar B-states and D-states is entirely ad hoc and can explain nothing unless it is embedded in a global assignment of syntax to the states of the subject (and perhaps of other subjects as well). The assignment of syntax to Skip's B-state and D-state in isolation from other states may appear to explain Skip's trip to the grocer. But I submit that this impression can only derive from mistaking the assignment of syntax for the assignment of contents. Note first that merely subsuming the B-state and D-state under the completely specific law "When the subject is in this particular B-state and this particular D-state, the subject tends to go to the grocer" is completely unexplanatory. Perhaps this appeal succeeds in citing the cause—the B-state and D-state—of the subject's behavior, but it does not explain the behavior. Note next that no greater progress toward explanation is made by appealing to a generalization of this specific law to B-states and D-states associated with a certain syntax *unless* the syntax is assigned in a nonarbitrary way. It would always be possible to *call* B-states and D-states that give rise to going to the grocer states with a certain syntax. Doing so would ensure that the general law mentioned above comes out true. But it would also make the law vacuously true and deprive appeal to the law of explanatory force. Thus, the syntax must be assigned on some systematic and principled basis. But it is hard to see what this basis could be other than an assignment of *contents* to the B-states and D-states. The syntax assigned must be some standard English expression of the contents assigned by commonsense psychology. But then the assignment of syntax is parasitic on the assignment of contents, and in the final analysis the syntactical explanation requires the assignment of contents.

A proponent of syntactical explanation might counter these points by claiming that there is a systematic and principled assignment of syntax to the B-states and D-states that is not parasitic on an ascription of contents: let the assignment of syntax be whatever assignment makes syntactically specified laws come out true in such a way as to optimize the explanation of behavior. But this counter runs into the response that there is no reason at all to believe that there is such an assignment, unless the assignment is the one that assigns the English expressions of the contents that make the laws of commonsense psychology come out true.

I do not wish to deny that it is possible to assign syntax to cognitive states or that this assignment could play a role in a set of laws governing behavior or that these laws could figure in the explanation of behavior. I do not even wish to deny that for some behavior, an explanation in terms of content is unavailable, and a syntactical explanation is the only one that can be given. Stephen Stich (1983, 56) gives a plausible example of such a case, the senile Mrs. T. Mrs. T has become senile in such a way that when asked whether McKinley was assassinated, she is able to answer "Yes," but when asked whether McKinley is dead, she is unable to say. As Stich points out, it is implausible to ascribe to Mrs. T the *belief* that McKinley was assassinated. For it is an indispensable part of that belief to believe that McKinley is dead, and Mrs. T clearly does not believe that McKinley is dead. At the same time, we can plausibly ascribe to Mrs. T some cognitive state, a B-state, associated with the syntax "McKinley was assassinated." And this B-state can figure in an explanation of Mrs. T's behavior. For example, suppose Mrs. T were offered a choice between two gifts. Gift *A* is a dollar if McKinley was assassinated and a hundred dollars if he was not assassinated. Gift *B* is a hundred dollars if McKinley was assassinated and a dollar if he was not. We could predict that Mrs. T would choose gift *B*, and we could explain her choice by appeal to her B-state. The ascription of the *belief* that McKinley was assassinated could play no role in our prediction or explanation, since we do not think that she has this belief.

All this seems quite right and important, but note that in the case of Mrs. T the syntax we assign is evidently parasitic on a prior assignment of beliefs with content. We would not be able to assign the syntax "McKinley was assassinated" to Mrs. T's B-state had we not already assigned the content that McKinley was assassinated to a belief that is an ancestor of the current B-state. To be sure, this is a content that the B-state does not have (or no longer has); and it is plausible enough to conclude from this that the B-state is not (or is no longer) a belief. But this does not change the fact that we assign the syntax to the B-state in virtue of having assigned a certain content to a belief. This is at least a fact about how we go about assigning the syntax, but I am inclined to think it is more than that. I am inclined to think that the assignment of syntax is essentially parasitic on the assignment of contents.

Now a proponent of syntactical explanation might say that we could give a syntactical explanation of Mrs. T's choice between the gifts even if Mrs. T had never had the belief that McKinley was assassinated. All that is required is that she answer "Yes" to the question "Was McKinley assassinated?" For this reason, the assignment of syntax cannot be parasitic on the assignment of contents. I do not wish to deny that this could be true of a small number of B-states. But I do not see how it could be *systematically* true. I do not see, for example, how Mrs. T could so much as *answer* the question "Was McKinley assassinated?" if she had no beliefs. For answering that question requires such beliefs as that a question has been posed, that it has a certain content, that an answer is being given, and so on. Perhaps some sense could be made of a being who said "Yes" to certain questions without answering them, and perhaps a syntactical account could be given of the verbal behavior of that being. Perhaps such an explanation would pertain to cases of autism, for example. But it would be exceedingly implausible to suppose that the form of explanation of such behavior carries over to normal human beings. It would be preposterous to think that what goes on in such cases is much like what goes on in normal human behavior. I maintain, therefore, that syntax can be nonparasitically assigned only to a few B-states; elsewhere it must coincide with the current or one-time assignment of contents to beliefs.

These remarks seem to me enough to cast doubt on a syntactical explanation of behavior in the absence of the ascription of beliefs and desires. Explaining behavior plausibly requires ascribing beliefs and desires and hence contents to beliefs and desires.[1] The argument from explaining behavior may assume as much. This spot in the argument turns out not to be as vulnerable as it might have seemed.

(2) Let us move, then, to the other vulnerable spot in the argument from explaining behavior. The argument claims that the contents ascribed to beliefs and desires have *correspondence* truth-conditions. One might reject this claim on the ground that we can explain behavior by referring to beliefs and desires without ascribing contents with correspondence truth-conditions. For we can ascribe beliefs and desires by *projection*, and this requires only an ascription of contents with deflationary truth-conditions (Stich 1983, 149-183, Goldman 1992).

In projecting beliefs and desires, one ascribes to others the beliefs and desires one would have in their circumstances. And it turns out that although projection ascribes contents with truth-conditions, the truth-conditions it ascribes are not correspondence but deflationary truth-conditions.[2]

Return to the case of Skip. I explain why Skip goes to the grocer by referring to his desire that he acquire food and his belief that by going to the grocer, he will acquire food. According to projectivism about content ascription, I ascribe the belief and the desire, with their contents, by *projecting* my own psychology onto Skip. I put myself in Skip's shoes by imagining which beliefs and desires would lead me to go to the grocer (given that I have the other relevant features that I know Skip to have in this situation). Suppose assigning beliefs and desires is a matter of projecting one's own psychology onto the subject in this way. Then, it might be inferred, when I say that Skip believes that by going to the grocer, he will acquire food, I am simply saying that Skip has a belief like the one that I would express by saying "By going to the grocer, I will acquire food."

Now this projectivist account of ascribing contents has significance for the argument from explaining behavior. For on a projectivist ascription of beliefs and desires, the contents ascribed have only deflationary truth-conditions. The contents are ascribed by the sentences that I would use to express states comparable to Skip's. I imagine which of my beliefs and desires would lead me to go to the grocer, and I ascribe the appropriate belief and desire to Skip. But the contents of the belief and desire are determined in the way that I ascribe contents to my own beliefs and desires. And I do this by considering how I would verbally express the belief and desire. The sentence "*p*" used to ascribe content need only have the truth-conditions that *p*—deflationary truth-conditions. Not only is it a sentence in my language, English, but the ascription of beliefs and desires to Skip explicitly relates Skip to my beliefs. That is, in projectivist ascription of beliefs and desires, which beliefs and desires Skip has are determined by a relation to the ascriber.

Thus, projectivist ascription works in such a way that the ascription relates the ascribed beliefs and desires to the ascriber. So if we ascribe beliefs and desires by projection, the correspondence theorist cannot protest that the explanation of the subject's behavior must not relate the subject to the explainer. If the explanation of behavior is projectivist, then the correspondence theorist is debarred from the objection that the truth-conditions ascribed cannot be deflationary because deflationary truth-conditions relate the beliefs and desires to the explainer. On the contrary, this is exactly what projectivist explanation requires. The argument that the truth-conditions ascribed in explaining behavior must be correspondence truth-conditions thus comes to grief. In short, projectivist explanation of behavior may ascribe beliefs and desires and may assign them contents and truth-conditions without any commitment to their having correspondence truth-conditions.

I find this projectivist reply to the argument from explaining behavior wanting. For on a pure projectivist account of the ascription of beliefs and desires, the ascription of beliefs and desires does not allow us to *explain* behavior, even if it allows us to predict behavior. The explanation of behavior must be left to *nonprojectivist* ascriptions of beliefs and desires—hence to ascriptions of beliefs and desires that involve ascribing contents with nondeflationary and presumably correspondence truth-conditions.

I say that projectivist ascriptions of beliefs and desires might allow us to predict but not explain behavior because projectivist assignments are too lean to do any explanatory work. For in projectivist ascriptions, there is something *incidental* about the relation between the states ascribed and the syntax that expresses my state. The syntactical way in which contents are ascribed to the subject's beliefs prevents the contents from playing a role in explaining the subject's behavior. It is this syntactical ascription of contents that affords deflationary truth-conditions for projectivist ascriptions. But this very syntactical ascription foils a projectivist explanation of behavior.

Consider a simple comparative explanation. Machine *A* delivers bubblegum when a dime is inserted. What explains this event? Well, we know that another machine, machine *B*, that delivers bubblegum when a dime is inserted works by a system of gears. Can we explain the behavior of machine *A* by saying that it is in a sequence of internal states like the ones machine *B* is in when it exhibits similar behavior, and the latter sequence—in machine *B*—is a sequence of gear turns? Certainly we can. But this amounts to an *explanation* (as opposed to a way of predicting behavior) only if we are willing to say not merely that machine *A* is in some unspecified way similar to machine *B* but also that its sequence of internal states is actually a sequence of gear turns. Hence, the explanation here is not merely comparative but comparative in such a way that the internal workings of machine *B* are ascribed to machine *A*. Attributing a similarity between the machines gives only the *illusion* of an explanation until we ascribe states to the machine whose behavior is explained (machine *A*, in this case) that are like the states of the other machine (machine *B*) *in the respects that provide an explanation of the behavior of that other machine.*

A similar point holds for psychological explanation. It is no explanation of Skip's behavior to say that he does what I would do were I in certain states that I would verbally express by certain sentences *unless* referring to my being in these states would explain my similar behavior. Yet surely the mere fact that I would *verbally express* my state by a certain sentence would be incidental to the causal explanation of my going to the grocer. What would cause me to go to the grocer is a certain belief, and the fact that I would express that belief by a certain sentence would play no role in the causal relation between my belief and my going to the grocer. My talk—the verbal expression of my belief—would be a mere *consequence* or epiphenomenon of my belief and play no part in the causal chain that explains my trip to the grocer. It is quite plausible that what explains Skip's trip to the grocer is something like what would explain my behavior (though in fact this is plausible only if Skip is assumed psychologically similar to me). But the explanation of Skip's behavior is then whatever would explain my behavior, and this has nothing to do with syntactically defined contents. If the explanation of Skip's behavior has to do with the contents of my beliefs—and it is hard to escape the view that it does—then the contents involved in the explanation cannot be ascribed merely because they are expressed by the sentences I would use to express verbally my state. My ascribing the contents does not essentially relate the belief and desire ascribed to Skip to me.

My conclusion is that projectivist ascriptions of beliefs and desires cannot explain behavior. In saying this I do not wish to denigrate the value of projecting the contents of our beliefs and desires onto others. For one thing, projection may still be useful for *predicting* behavior, and that is no small matter. Given that Skip has certain beliefs and desires, I predict Skip's behavior by imagining what I would do if I had those beliefs and desires. For another thing, my *method* of nonprojectively ascribing beliefs and desires could still involve projection. That is, given Skip's behavior, I could infer his beliefs and desires by a method of projection. I ascribe to Skip the beliefs and desires that would cause me to behave as he does. Of course it would not follow from this that the *conditions* of belief and desire are merely projectivist. If what I have argued is correct, those conditions are not projectivist.

These points seem to me enough to do in the projectivist reply to the argument from explaining behavior. Neither the projectivist reply nor the syntactical reply is effective against the argument. We may conclude that the argument makes a presumptive case for ascribing truth-conditions in explaining behavior. The explanatory argument of course turns on whether truth can implicitly involve a relation to a truth-ascriber.

Let us note that if the argument from explaining behavior succeeds, then we must ascribe correspondence truth-conditions to *every* proposition that could be ascribed as a content in explaining human behavior (or perhaps in explaining any intentional behavior whatever, human or otherwise). I am inclined to believe that this class of propositions includes every proposition expressible by a human being in any natural language, actual or possible. That's a lot of propositions. Not all, perhaps, but the correspondence theory that emerges from the argument is highly general. It characterizes a notion of truth that applies to a vast range of propositions. Moreover, the notion of truth it characterizes is the ordinary notion we (usually tacitly) employ in ascribing beliefs. The argument from explaining behavior thus establishes that the ordinary notion of truth is a correspondence notion and applies to a vast range of propositions, including at least all propositions expressible in a human language.

Defining T-reliability

A second argument for the correspondence theory is that we need a correspondence notion of truth even to *define* the reliability of human beliefs in anything like the sense in which reliability is ascribed in everyday life and in that portion of psychological science that studies human cognitive performance. I will use Field's (1986, 89-99) term "T-reliability" to refer to the kind of reliability in question, but without assuming at the outset just what T-reliability amounts to.

We should begin by noting that it is not possible to give a purely *syntactical* definition of T-reliability. Such a definition would of course skirt a correspondence notion of truth-conditions because it would avoid employing *any* notion of truth-conditions. But a purely syntactical definition is not to be had. To see this, consider the natural syntactical definition:

> A person *S* is T-reliable on a topic just in case, for any B-state of *S* assigned a sentence on that topic, *p*

where "*p*" expresses the proposition expressed by the relevant sentence. Here we employ the notion of a B-state—a cognitive state playing a causal role like that of a belief—but to which only uninterpreted syntax is assigned, not content or truth-conditions. This definition does not avoid truth-conditions for two reasons. First, it makes use of the notion of a *topic*. But saying that a sentence is *on a topic* is equivalent to saying that it has a *content* that belongs to that topic. Hence, the definition covertly employs the notion of content and thus truth-conditions. Second, it employs the notion of a proposition, since it identifies "*p*" by saying that "*p*" is a sentence that expresses a certain proposition. Thus, the definition (not so covertly) ascribes propositions and truth-conditions to the sentences assigned to the B-states. So the definition is not purely syntactical.

It is tempting to try a *deflationary* definition of T-reliability (Ramsey 1927). The idea would be that

> A person is T-reliable on a topic just in case for any <*p*> on the topic, if the person believes that *p*, then *p*.

As it turns out, however, this definition falls short of encapsulating the notion of T-reliability employed in everyday life and psychology.

Before explaining why, I would like to warn against one tempting objection to the definition. One might imagine that if my earlier remarks on the explanation of behavior hold, the definition of T-reliability *obviously* cannot employ a deflationary notion of truth-conditions; it must employ a correspondence notion. For it employs talk of beliefs with contents, and—one might suppose—by my earlier argument, such beliefs have truth-conditions and in particular correspondence truth-conditions. But despite my argument, the talk of beliefs with contents here does *not* obviously require talk of correspondence truth-conditions. For it may yet be that a *projectivist* notion of the contents of beliefs is enough to define T-reliability, and as we have seen, the projectivist notion does not involve correspondence truth-conditions. I did argue earlier that we need a nonprojectivist notion of truth-conditions *for purposes of explaining behavior*. But we have not yet established that the notion of T-reliability must be employed to explain behavior in a way that involves correspondence truth-conditions. So we have not yet shown that the notion of T-reliability requires correspondence truth-conditions. We will have to wait to clear this up until we discuss the uses of the notion of T-reliability.

Nevertheless, I do wish to suggest here that we need a notion of correspondence truth-conditions to define T-reliability in its everyday use, as well as its use in scientific psychology, quite apart from whether the notion is employed to explain behavior. To see why this is so, we must recognize that the definition of T-reliability above is inadequate for what we want to say, and inadequate in such a way that it must be revised using a nondeflationary and, it seems, correspondence notion of truth. For we want to be able to assign T-reliability to cognizers whose beliefs have as contents propositions *not expressible in English*. And the proposed deflationary definition of T-reliability fails to capture the kind of T-reliability we wish to assign. For the quantifier "for any <*p*>" in the deflationary definition is a *substitutional* quantifier.

Recall that a substitutional quantifier over propositions, "for all <*p*>," ranges only over propositions *expressible in English*. Using the deflationary definition of T-reliability, we can say that a subject is T-reliable regarding a topic when the subject's beliefs are mostly true. But we can say this, employing the deflationary notion of T-reliability, only if every proposition belonging to the relevant topic is *expressible in English*. We could not say (or deny), for example, that *God* is T-reliable. Thus, if we are to capture our everyday notion of T-reliability and be able to say what we want to say, we need to revise the deflationary definition of T-reliability by changing from a substitutional to an *objectual* quantifier. But we cannot just repeat the same definition using an objectual quantifier. This would involve us in saying:

> A person *S* is T-reliable on a topic just in case, for any object *x*, if *S* believes *x*, then *x*.

But of course this is gibberish: the name of an object like "Pegasus" cannot appear in the blank in the expression "*S* believes that ___" ("*S* believes that Pegasus") or "if . . . , then ___." So instead we have to say something like:

> A person *S* is T-reliable on a topic just in case, for any proposition $<p>$ on the topic, if *S* believes that *p*, then $<p>$ is true.

But this new definition of T-reliability employs a *nondeflationary* notion of truth, since the proposition variable ranges over propositions not expressible in English. Only a proposition variable ranging over all propositions would enable us to say (or deny) that God is T-reliable. But what could the nondefla-tionary notion of truth employed here be but a *correspondence* notion (once the nondeflationary alternatives of pragmatism and the coherence theory of truth have been ruled out)? I would suggest, then, that we need a nondeflationary, correspondence notion of truth even to define T-reliability in its everyday or scientific use. And this is something we need quite apart from any role T-reliability might play in explaining behavior.

T-reliability in Inference from Testimony

In light of the preceding argument for the correspondence theory, it might be granted that the notion of T-reliability requires truth-conditions and indeed correspondence truth-conditions, but it might be noted at the same time that we have not yet shown the need for a notion of T-reliability. Thus, even if the correspondence theory characterizes the notion of truth-conditions employed in our everyday and scientific notion of T-reliability, it does not follow that we need a correspondence notion of truth for any important intellectual work. The notion of T-reliability that requires correspondence truth-conditions might, for all we have shown, be intellectually idle. Perhaps the deflationary notion of T-reliability will serve all the purposes we need served.

This objection is fair enough. In rejoinder, we must show two things: that a notion of T-reliability is needed for some important intellectual purpose, and that one is needed that either employs a nonprojectivist, hence correspondence, notion of belief contents or otherwise applies to subjects for whom the earlier deflationary definition of T-reliability is inadequate.

To show that a notion of T-reliability that employs a correspondence notion of truth is needed for some important purpose, we must argue that we need a notion of T-reliability employing a notion of belief and hence content, and that this notion involves correspondence truth-conditions. In fact, we need such a notion of T-reliability for several purposes, of which I will be able to discuss only one in detail—the use of the notion in our inferences on the basis of testimony. This case for a notion of T-reliability needing correspondence truth-conditions might be called the *argument from testimony*.

As an initial step in the argument, we may observe with Field that when we make use of testimony, as we extensively do, we (sometimes, at least) infer the attested conclusion from the reliability of the testifier. I ask a cabdriver which way I turn to get to Clark, and I infer from the answer—in the presence of my belief that the driver is reliable on the topic of Chicago streets—that I should go west. But there is no way this inference can proceed without my employing a notion of T-reliability involving belief, hence content, hence truth-conditions. For the inference depends on connecting the attested conclusion with the reliability of the testifier, and that requires connecting the truth of the proposition believed by the cabdriver with the tendency of the propositions the driver believes to be true. In general, inferring an attested proposition involves connecting it with the T-reliability of the testifier. And this notion of T-reliability employs the notions of belief, content, and truth-conditions. The inference takes this form:

> Testifier *T* is T-reliable on the topic—i.e., generally believes what is true on the topic.
> Testifier *T* believes that *p*.
> Therefore, probably, *p*.

The notion of T-reliability employed in this argument must be such that the inference connects the tendency to truth of the testifier's beliefs on the topic with the truth of *p*. But that means that the inference from testimony requires the subject to employ a truth-conditional notion of reliability.

The second step of the argument from testimony involves inquiring into whether the truth-conditional notion of T-reliability in the inference employs a *correspondence* notion of truth-conditions. Presumably, the notion of T-reliability here employs a notion of content with correspondence truth-conditions if the reference to the contents of beliefs here employs a nonprojectivist notion of belief content. In fact the present notion of T-reliability must employ a nonprojectivist notion of content. For it must apply to subjects for whom a projectivist notion of content does not work. The reason is that when one infers one's belief *p* from testimony, one may infer it on the basis of an ascription of reliability that ranges over beliefs inexpressible by any sentence one could use. Indeed, one may ascribe reliability that ranges over propositions not expressible in English. To be sure, when one judges the reliability of the subject by checking the truth-value of the propositions concerning the topic on which the subject has beliefs, one may employ one's own beliefs in propositions on the topic. For one may rely on one's own beliefs on the topic to verify the T-reliability of the subject. And of course one's own beliefs are (by and large) expressible in English, so that many of the beliefs on the topic must likewise be expressible in English. But first, checking the reliability of the subject by relying on one's own beliefs on the topic is not the only way to check the subject's reliability: one may also employ one's theoretical beliefs (e.g., about evolution) to judge the reliability of the subject. In this way, one may judge the reliability of the subject even if many or all propositions on the topic are not propositions one can express. Second, one may infer the subject's T-reliability from a relatively small sample of instances. In this case, too, one need not be able to express all beliefs on the topic. So the notion of T-reliability may apply to subjects to whom one cannot ascribe content by projection. Thus, the notion of T-reliability in the inference from testimony employs a correspondence notion of truth-conditions.

Besides inference from testimony, there are other purposes to which we put the notion of T-reliability. We need the notion to infer that we can rely on a subject to perform given kinds of tasks—e.g., bake a cake or drive a cab—even though we cannot foresee which propositions the subject will have to believe to perform those tasks or even whether those propositions will be expressible by us or expressible in English. Here it is even more obvious than in the case of testimony that a projectivist notion of content will not suffice. The relevant notion of T-reliability employs a correspondence notion of truth-conditions. (We also need a notion of reliability (though not quite T-reliability) employing a correspondence notion of truth-conditions to define knowledge and justified belief. But this is not a matter I can address here (see Schmitt 1992).) In all, we have enough basis for concluding that a correspondence notion of truth is needed for the notion of T-reliability as it is used in our everyday thinking.

T-reliability in Explaining Successful Practices

A fourth argument for correspondence truth, proposed by Field (1986, 89-99), is that a correspondence notion of truth comes into play when the notion of T-reliability is used to explain successful practices. Often what enables people to succeed in fulfilling their desires in a regular way (e.g., to make money on the stock market or repair automobiles) is their T-reliability on the relevant topics (on stock investing or auto repair). But the power of T-reliability to enable people to make money or repair cars cannot turn on anything about us, the explainers; the explanation of success cannot be projectivist. Hence, the notion of T-reliability employs a correspondence notion of truth.

I find this a persuasive argument for correspondence truth. I need only forestall here a possible misunderstanding about the explanation of success. In Chapter 1, I rejected the pragmatic argument for realism. As this argument would have it, we need to postulate mind-independent objects to explain our success in certain practices. My rejection of the argument might be thought to clash with my endorsement of the present argument for a correspondence theory of truth. One might think that consistency requires me to reject the present explanatory argument for the correspondence theory as well. But please recall the reason the pragmatic argument broke down: nothing in it secured the mind-independent existence of objects. Here the claim is not that objects are mind-independent but that the causal explanation of success has to do with interactions between objects and their environments, however these may be constituted. Consequently, I may reject the pragmatic argument for realism without also rejecting the present explanatory argument for the correspondence theory.

We have reviewed several arguments for the correspondence theory: the argument from explaining behavior, from defining

T-reliability, from using the notion of T-reliability in inference from testimony and in reliance on others to perform tasks, and from the role of the notion of T-reliability in explaining successful practices. All four arguments turn, albeit in different ways, on the fact that we employ, and (in the case of all but the second argument) need to employ, a notion of truth that does not make truth a relation to the truth-ascriber. The correspondence notion of truth is serviceable where the deflationary notion cannot be. All four arguments seem to me forceful, and together they make a substantial case for the correspondence theory. I believe that unless there is some equally substantial objection to the correspondence theory, the arguments are sufficient to warrant acceptance of the theory, especially in light of the objections to the alternative theories, many of which also turn on their making truth a relation to the truth-ascriber.

To reach a final judgment about the correspondence theory, then, we must consider objections to the correspondence theory. Since most of these touch only specific versions of the theory, I will turn to these versions and review objections as we go. (For further review of versions of and objections to the correspondence theory, see O'Connor 1975, Vision 1988, and Kirkham 1992, 119-140.)

II. Versions of the Correspondence Theory

Moore's Correspondence Theory

G. E. Moore (1953) offers a simple fact correspondence theory, applied to beliefs:

> The belief that *p* is true just in case there is a fact to which this belief corresponds.

> The belief that p corresponds only to the fact that p.
> The belief that p is false just in case there is no fact to which it corresponds.

This theory, unlike the other correspondence theories we will consider, makes correspondence a *logical* relation between propositions and facts: a belief is true when it corresponds to the facts in the sense that it has the *same content* as some fact.

At this point, it is natural to lodge a protest against Moore's theory. The fact that p, according to this protest, is nothing other than the truth of the proposition that p. Hence, Moore's theory defines truth in terms of not a substantive correspondence but an identity: a belief is true just in case the truth of the proposition believed holds. But of course this definition is circular. However, Moore could with some justice balk at the claim that the fact that p is the truth of the proposition that p. Among other reasons for denying this, Moore could point to usage: we do not say that the truth of a proposition obtains, as we say that a fact obtains. Nor do we say that there is a truth of the proposition, as we say that there is a fact. The charge of circularity is therefore unconvincing.

One might instead object to Moore's theory on the ground that it entails that there are facts. Now, to avoid commitment to facts, Moore could retreat to a version of the theory expressed in terms of states of affairs: a belief is true just in case there is a state of affairs to which it corresponds. Moore might concede that it is reasonable enough to doubt whether there are any facts, but he could insist that to doubt whether there are states of affairs is strange.

Unfortunately for this way of responding to the charge of commitment to facts, it is somewhat more difficult to define the correspondence between beliefs and states of affairs than it is to define that between beliefs and facts. If Moore lets the belief that p correspond to the state of affairs that p, then one might legitimately object that his new talk of states of affairs is really no different from talk of facts. The advantage of moving from facts to states of affairs was supposed to be that it is less tendentious to commit oneself to there being states of affairs than to there being facts. But this difference between states of affairs and facts holds only for run-of-the-mill states of affairs like *the table's being blue*; it does not hold for questionable ones like the state of affairs *that the table is blue*. It is no more plausible to affirm the existence of the latter state of affairs than it is to affirm the existence of the fact that the table is blue. Of course, the force of the present objection to Moore turns on whether there are grounds for rejecting the existence of facts. The grounds that are nowadays taken most seriously are reasons for relativism about truth. But we may ignore these at this late stage of the game. I am inclined to think that Moore would do best to stand his ground here and maintain the existence of facts. While it may be more tendentious to affirm the existence of facts than to affirm the existence of certain states of affairs, it is by no means ridiculous to do so. And I doubt whether there are any persuasive arguments *against* the existence of facts.

A greater threat to Moore's theory is that it entails Bivalence. For either there is a fact to which the belief that <*p*> corresponds or there is no such fact. And in this case, it follows that either <*p*> is true or <*p*> is false. But as we argued in Chapter 5, Bivalence is mistaken; it runs afoul of borderline vagueness.

This objection does tell against Moore. How forceful we take the objection to be against a Moorean approach to truth depends on how satisfying we find the following Moorean alternative account of truth. This alternative involves distinguishing two ways in which a proposition can correspond to the facts. A proposition can correspond *positively* to the facts, or it can correspond *negatively* to the facts. Truth is then defined as positive correspondence and falsity as negative correspondence:

> <*p*> is false just in case there is a fact to which <*p*> negatively corresponds.

Positive correspondence is understood in the manner of Moore's original definition of truth.

This Moorean alternative does avoid the Bivalence objection to Moore's theory. For a proposition can now be neither true nor false. The difficulty with this alternative is that it gives us no way to understand negative correspondence. That notion is so far undefined. Is there any satisfying way to define it? Clearly, it cannot be given a *logical* definition of this sort:

> <*p*> negatively corresponds to a fact *F* just in case *F* is the fact that not-*p*.

For then Bivalence would come back again, since it is either a fact that *p* or a fact that not-*p* for each <*p*>. Negative correspondence must be defined in some other way. It is clear that Bivalence can be avoided only by a *nonlogical* definition, one that does *not* make its being a fact that not-*p* entail that <*p*> is false. But now we are quite far from the logical origins of Moore's view. Other correspondence theories have the important advantage over Moore's of making correspondence a nonlogical relation.

Austin's Correspondence Theory

One such theory is J. L. Austin's (1950):

> A statement *S* is true just in case *S* is correlated by demonstrative conventions with a state of affairs *s* of a type correlated by descriptive conventions with the sentence used in making the statement *S*.

As you can see, Austin takes states of affairs, rather than facts or objects and their properties, to be the items in the world to which statements must correspond. The choice of states of affairs renders irrelevant any objection to the effect that there are no facts. And the appeal to a nonlogical correspondence relation makes it possible to avoid Bivalence.

Austin takes *statements* rather than propositions or sentences to be the bearers of truth-values. We *make* statements by uttering sentences (or sentence-tokens), whereas we *express* propositions, also by uttering sentences. Austin's choice of statements as the primary bearers of truth-values is controversial, but again this choice need not detain us here, since nothing that matters for our purposes will turn on it.

Austin's theory assumes that there are *demonstrative* conventions that correlate particular *statements* (made in uttering sentence-tokens) with particular states of affairs. He also assumes that there are *descriptive* conventions that correlate *sentences* (that is, sentence-types) used to make statements with types of states of affairs. For example, let us suppose that on an occasion I make the statement that I am sitting in Gregory Hall, and this statement is true. This statement is correlated by demonstrative conventions with the state of affairs my sitting in Gregory Hall. The sentence-type "I am sitting in Gregory Hall" is correlated by descriptive conventions with the type of state of affairs the utterer's sitting in Gregory Hall. The particular statement on that occasion that I am sitting in Gregory Hall is true on Austin's theory because it is correlated by the demonstrative conventions with the state of affairs my sitting in Gregory Hall, a state of affairs that is of a type (the type: the utterer's sitting in Gregory Hall) correlated by the descriptive conventions with the sentence-type "I am sitting in Gregory Hall."

Austin's theory has been challenged in several ways. As I have mentioned, his choice of statements as bearers of truth-values is controversial (Strawson 1950). The presupposition that there are demonstrative and descriptive conventions has also been challenged (Vision 1988; see Johnson 1992, 182-188, for defense). But from the standpoint of our treatment of the correspondence theory in this chapter, the main problem with Austin's theory of truth, and indeed, with all other fact and state of affairs theories of truth, is that the notion of truth it defines cannot do the job a correspondence notion needs to do if we are to employ it to explain behavior and account for the role of the notion of T-reliability in explaining successful practices. The need for a correspondence notion is based in large measure on the need for a notion of truth that performs these explanatory tasks. But the notion defined by Austin's theory cannot perform these tasks.

The key point is that a theory of truth on which the notion of truth performs these tasks must assign truth-conditions *compositionally*. Yet Austin's theory and other fact and state of affairs theories do not do so. I will focus first on the compositional assignment of truth-conditions to the sentences of a language rather than to beliefs or propositions. A compositional assignment of truth-conditions is possible only if the language has a compositional syntax—that is, compound sentences are composed of simple sentences, and simple sentences are composed of terms. We must assume that the simplest or *atomic* sentences (e.g., "Fido is a dog") are composed of a term (in the present example, a proper name, "Fido") and a predicate ("is a dog"). Terms include not only proper names but other linguistic subjects (e.g., pronouns like "I" and "she"). *Compound* sentences ("Fido is a dog, and Woody is a cat") are composed of atomic sentences ("Fido is a dog" and "Woody is a cat") connected by logical connectives (in this case "and," but other connectives include "or" and "if, then"). (We may leave aside here compound sentences involving quantifiers like "for all.")

A compositional assignment of truth-conditions to the sentences of the language will assign truth-conditions to the compound sentences as a function of the truth-conditions of the simpler sentences of which they are composed. For example, "Fido is a dog, and Woody is a cat" will be assigned the truth-value true just in case both "Fido is a dog" is true and "Woody is a cat" is true. The atomic sentences will, for their part, be assigned truth-conditions as a function of the referents of the terms (e.g., "Fido" refers to a particular dog, Fido) and the extensions of the predicates ("is a dog" has as its extension the set of all dogs). Thus, "Fido is a dog" will be assigned the truth-value true just when the object to which the name "Fido" refers actually belongs to the extension of the predicate "is a dog" (i.e., belongs to the set of all dogs). All this gives an idea of a compositional assignment of truth-conditions to sentences. We may understand a compositional assignment to beliefs or propositions analogously. We treat the contents of beliefs and desires as composed in a manner exactly analogous to the manner in which the sentences that express these contents are composed. We analyze atomic contents as being composed of something analogous to terms and predicates, and compound contents as composed of atomic contents connected by analogues of logical connectives. It is by no means uncontroversial that beliefs or propositions have a compositional structure analogous to that of sentences. But if they do not, then correspondence truth of the sort for which we have argued will not apply to them directly. It will have to apply indirectly, in virtue of the relation between sentences and beliefs (or propositions).

Now, why must a correspondence theory assign truth-conditions compositionally? The answer is that only a compositional assignment can do the job of explaining behavior and accounting for the role of T-reliability in explaining successful practices. To take the case of explaining behavior, the explanation of Skip's going to the grocer requires an assignment of truth-conditions to beliefs and desires that recognizes that a belief and a desire can each have as a component of its content the *same* atomic sentence and that the belief and desire issue in an action in virtue of this overlapping content. The assignment of truth-conditions must treat the belief and the desire as having the same sentence as a component. Otherwise there is no explanation of *why* the desire, with its content about acquiring food, gives rise to going to the grocer in the presence of a belief that is also about acquiring food. If the contents of the desire and the belief are treated as unitary rather than composed, it is not possible to explain how the desire and belief combine to give rise to the action. Moreover, if we are to see the action as reasonable, then we must treat the relation between the belief, desire, and action as something like an argument in which the contents of the belief and desire are premises, and a description of the action is a conclusion:

> If I acquire food, I go to the grocer. (An implication of the belief)
> I acquire food. (Desire)
> Therefore, I go to the grocer. (A description of the action)

The truth-condition assigned the compound sentence that expresses the belief-content must be at least in part a function of the truth-conditions of its atomic components.

Now up to this point, there is nothing that should worry a fact correspondence theorist. Since the atomic sentences are treated as units, the facts that correspond to them may be treated as units. But this is not the end of the story. For similar reasoning shows that the correspondence theorist must treat *atomic sentences* as having compositional truth-conditions as well. One point is that to explain why Skip's belief and desire give rise to his behavior, we must see the term "I" appearing in the content of both the belief and the desire as referring to the same person, Skip. Otherwise there is no explanation of why the belief and desire give rise to the behavior of the referrent of "I," Skip. To be sure, we can still explain the action designated by "my going to the grocer" as caused by the belief expressed by "By going to the grocer I will acquire food" and the desire expressed by "I acquire food." But our ability to explain this falls short of an ability to explain a number of other things we take ourselves to be able to explain.

For example, it falls short of an ability to explain Skip's going to the grocer as caused by the belief and desire. To explain that, given the explanation we already have, we would have to know that "my going to the grocer" refers to Skip's going to the grocer. But that requires knowing that "my" is a possessive adjective for Skip's. To know that, we need to have an account of the reference of the terms. That does not quite commit us to saying that the truth-conditions of the contents of beliefs and desires must be given by the referents of terms and extensions of predicates. But there is an additional argument for that. We need such a compositional assignment of truth-conditions if we are to explain why *Skip* went to the grocer by appeal to a belief and a desire about Skip. To explain this, we must see the term "I" in the expression of the content of the belief and desire as referring to the same entity, Skip. But this requires a compositional account of truth-conditions that goes down below the level of atomic sentences.

There are other points in favor of a compositional assignment of truth-conditions. These points do not emerge directly from the tasks of a correspondence theory, but they do bear on the format of a correspondence theory, since they concern the structure of truth-conditions. I will mention one such point concerning inference from one belief to another, rather than practical reasoning from a belief and desire to an action. We must sometimes treat terms in the contents of different beliefs as referring to the same object in order to explain the subject's reasoning. If I believe that all beavers have flat tails, and I believe that this is a beaver, then I may infer that this has a flat tail. There are certain things about such inferences that must be explained by treating the latter two beliefs as having an atomic content composed of a term and a predicate. For example, suppose we wish to explain why I infer that this is a beaver rather than that *that* is a beaver. Presumably the reason is that my prior beliefs are about *this* beaver and not that beaver. We explain this by saying that my prior beliefs contain a term referring to this beaver. But obviously saying so requires treating the terms as referring. And the reference must get into the truth-conditions of the beliefs, since the contents of the beliefs play a crucial role in the causal explanation of the inference. Thus, it is necessary to relate the terms in these two beliefs. Otherwise, we cannot explain how the first belief—that all beavers have flat tails—bears on the second two in such a way as to cause the subject to make the inference. If we may paint a graphic picture of the inference, the first belief may be expressed roughly by the sentence "If this is a beaver, then it has a flat tail." The second belief is expressed by the sentence "This is a beaver." To get to the third belief, that this has a flat tail, we must treat the term "this" in the expression of the third belief as referring to the beaver referred to by "this" in the expression of the second belief. But treating the terms this way requires a compositional view of the contents of these sentences, in particular, a view on which the smallest components are smaller than atomic sentences. This does not show that a theory of truth must give a compositional assignment of truth-conditions. It does show, however, that a theory of truth that gives a compositional assignment will have one advantage over a theory that does not. For it will be able to explain inference in the manner just described.

We have enough reason here to reject a fact or state of affairs version of the correspondence theory in favor of a version that gives a compositional assignment of truth-conditions.

Field's Correspondence Theory

One such version is that of Hartry Field (1972). Though Field never attempts more than a sketch of his version of the correspondence theory, certain elements of it have been worked out by others in enough detail to confer the title "theory" (see Devitt 1981).

Field's theory is compositional in the right way. It assigns truth-conditions compositionally, first assigning referents to names and extensions to predicates and then truth-values to atomic sentences and, truth-functionally, to complex sentences. The theory thus avoids the primary difficulty with fact and state of affairs versions of the correspondence theory.

To understand Field's theory, it will help to begin where Field does—with Alfred Tarski's important *semantic conception of truth* (Tarski 1956; for a thorough and careful review of Tarski's conception of truth, see Kirkham 1992, 141-210). Tarski undertook to define truth-in-a-language-*L* for formal languages of certain kinds. The point of Tarski's definition is to produce a theory of truth that entails all the T-sentences of the language, but in which the definiens contains no *semantic* expressions—i.e., no expressions like "refers," "denotes," or "the extension of a predicate." The reason why Tarski wished to avoid semantic expressions is that he hoped to provide a physicalist definition of truth—one that eliminated all semantic talk in favor of talk that could be employed by a "physicalist," one who regards the language of physics as the preferred way of talking about things. We need not worry here about just what a physicalist is supposed to be or what it means to prefer one way of talking about things to another. For we need not share Tarski's physicalist orientation to agree with him that a theory of truth ought to break out of the circle of semantic expressions of which "truth" is one of the primary examples. A definition of truth in terms of "refers" or "denotes" remains in a sense circular and less revealing than we desire a definition to be. The definition of truth ought to avoid semantic talk even if it does not employ physicalist talk.

This is not to insist that truth *must* be definable in nonsemantic terms. Perhaps it is not so definable. For several reasons, however, that is not an outcome to be desired. Most pertinent to our present purposes is the point that if there were no nonsemantical definition of truth, then we would not be able to account for the role of the notion of truth in the explanation of behavior. There is also the point that truth must be nonsemantically definable if we are to explain the supervenience of truth on nonsemantical properties. To say that truth supervenes on nonsemantical properties is to say that nonsemantical properties in some strong sense generate the truths. In particular, it is to say that if there were two possible worlds with the same nonsemantical properties, the same propositions would be *true* in each of these worlds. The problem is now that unless truth is nonsemantically definable, the supervenience of truth on nonsemantical properties must be an inexplicable, brute fact about the world. That would be both undesirable and implausible. It would be undesirable because it would reduce the size of the set of facts we are able to explain. And it would be implausible because it would be strange if it turned out that which truths there are were a matter distinct from the nonsemantical facts and yet were determined by which nonsemantical facts there are. This would be strange in much the way that it would be strange if it turned out that mental states were nonphysical and yet supervened on physical states: there would be no reason why precisely the same mental states should appear wherever the same physical states do. (Of course if truth were not an objective feature of the world but merely our projection on the world—as a result, for example, of some emotional reaction to it, or, more plausibly, as a result of the use of "true" as part of a system of verbal incentives for argument and consensus [as in Price 1988, 117-218], then there would be nothing strange here, since we would presumably project the same truths when we imagined the same nonsemantical facts. In this case, no definition of truth in nonsemantical terms would be needed. But I have assumed throughout this book, in line with pragmatism, coherentism, deflationism, and the correspondence theory, that truth is an objective feature of the world, in the relevant sense of "objective" and "feature." I will return to the question of nondescriptivist theories of truth in the next section.) In short, both our need to account for the supervenience of truth on nonsemantical properties and our need to account for the role of the notion of truth in the explanation of behavior call for a definition of truth in nonsemantical terms. We do well, therefore, to seek a nonsemantical definition and to surrender our effort only in the event of substantial evidence that no such definition is to be had.

To elaborate Tarski's semantic conception of truth, I will assume we are defining truth for a very simple language, *L*. Tarski's is a conception of truth-in-a-language-*L*, and for reasons I will go into below, truth is definable only in a metalanguage containing the language *L* (in our case, English augmented with some formal apparatus). Let *L* have two predicates, "F_1" and "F_2" (e.g., "a dog" and "a cat"), and two names, "a_1" and "a_2" ("Fido" and "Woody"). Tarski did not in fact define truth-in-*L* for a language *L* with names, but there is a natural way of extending his definition to cover such languages, and I will apply that extension here.

For purposes of illustration, we may limit ourselves to defining truth for the atomic sentences of *L*. The definition of truth for compound sentences would be more involved, but we need not develop it here. As we have identified *L*, it has four atomic sentences: "a_1 is F_1," "a_1 is F_2," "a_2 is F_1," and "a_2 is F_2." Tarski would define truth for the atomic sentences of *L* in this way:

Atomic sentence A is true just in case A = "a_1 is F_1" and the object denoted by "a_1" is F_1, or A = "a_1 is F_2" and the object denoted by "a_1" is F_2, or A = "a_2 is F_1" and the object denoted by "a_2" is F_1, or A= "a_2 is F_2" and the object denoted by "a_2" is F_2.

This definition does not yet eliminate the semantic expression "denoted," as required for Tarski's physicalist definition. Thus, the definition must be supplemented by a definition of denotation. Tarski would offer this definition:

x denotes y just in case (x = "a_1" and $y = a_1$) or (x = "a_2" and $y = a_2$).

This completes the definition of truth for the atomic sentences of L.

There are four drawbacks of Tarski's definition of truth-in-a-language. One is that it defines truth only for languages in which there are finitely many names and predicates and not for natural languages like English, which have infinitely many names and predicates. This is because the definition of truth for atomic sentences is disjunctive (i.e., of the form "p or q"), and there can be only finitely many disjuncts in a disjunction in a metalanguage like English; hence there can be only finitely many atomic sentences; hence only finitely many names and predicates. This finitary limitation is imposed by the format of Tarski's definition of truth.

A second drawback of Tarski's theory, already mentioned, is that it defines truth-in-language-L only in a metalanguage of which the language L is a *fragment*. One cannot understand the Tarskian definition of truth-in-L for a language L one does not speak. To see this, observe that in the definitions of truth and denotation, the names "a_1" and "a_2" and the predicates "F_1" and "F_2" are not merely mentioned in the definiens of the definition but *used* as part of the language in which the definition is stated. That is, they are employed as part of the metalanguage; hence they must be understood by one who understands the definition. One must speak the language *L* in order to understand Tarski's definition of truth-in-*L*. So the metalanguage must contain *L* as a part. Thus, the definition has the same drawback as a deflationary definition of truth for purposes of explaining behavior: it can assign truth-conditions only for propositions expressible in English (or another metalanguage that contains the language of the subject whose behavior is explained).

A third drawback of Tarski's definition, also already in evidence, is that it defines not truth, but truth-in-a-language. In other words, in explaining behavior one must employ a *different* definition of truth depending on the language of the subject whose behavior is explained. And of course this seems quite wrong. It is most implausible to suppose that the explanation of behavior must always vary with the language of the subject. On the contrary, it seems that for most forms of behavior, the explanation of the behavior would not vary with the language of the subject.

The fourth and most significant objection to Tarski's definition, raised by Field (1972), is that Tarski's theory does not provide an explanatory reduction of the concept of truth to physicalist concepts, even though it defines truth in terms of physicalist concepts. It does not provide an *explanatory* reduction of the concept of denotation to physicalist concepts. For it defines denotation by a list of assignments of terms to objects. A definition giving a genuine reduction would explain how the list is generated. One can sympathize with this objection even if one rejects Tarski's and Field's preference for a physicalist definition of truth. For even without this preference, the definition fails to capture any property that true sentences have in common. Merely giving a list of assignments of terms to objects does not identify what true sentences have in common and so does not capture the notion of truth.

Field proposes a way to amend Tarski's definition of truth to avoid these drawbacks. Restricting our attention again to atomic sentences, Field replaces Tarski's clause for atomic sentences with a clause according to which

> *A* is true just in case *A* = "*a* is *F*" for some name "*a*" and predicate "*F*," and "*F*" applies to the object denoted by "*a*."

If we are to eliminate semantic expressions from this definition, we must supplement it with definitions of *denotation* and *application*. Field proposes to define these, not by a list as above, but by a *causal theory* of application and denotation—a theory on which a name denotes an object when the name is appropriately related to the object.

A causal theory of denotation and application is perhaps not the only sort of theory that might suit the tasks of a correspondence theory. One popular alternative theory of denotation, the "description" theory, is, however, ruled out at least in its usual formulation. According to this theory, a name "*a*" denotes an object *x* just in case the meaning of that name consists of a set of descriptions and sufficiently many of these descriptions are true of *x*. The notion of "true of" that appears in this account of denotation is unfortunately the notion of application, and unless the latter notion can be given an account that does not employ the notion of truth, appeal to the description theory will be circular. I will not, however, adjudicate among theories of denotation and application but simply rely on the causal theory in what follows. Let it be noted that both the causal theory and the description theory of denotation and application leave open the choice between competing accounts of mental representation—covariation, interpretationist, and functionalist accounts—that might figure in the account of linguistic denotation (see Cummins 1989 for an insightful review of these accounts of mental representation).

Any of these accounts will do for the purposes the notion of truth must serve according to the arguments for the correspondence theory. What is required of them, as of the account of denotation, is only that the conditions of denotation they supply not make denotation a relation to us in the manner ruled out by the arguments for the correspondence theory. That is true of the causal and description theories, and of the aforementioned accounts of mental representation as well.

The basic idea of a causal theory of denotation is that a name denotes an object when our use of the name is suitably causally related to the object:

> A name "*a*" denotes an object *x* just in case our use of "*a*" is suitably causally related to *x*.

The name "Aristotle" refers to a certain Greek philosopher who lived in the fourth century B.C.E. because our use of this name is the product of a chain of uses of the name (or in this case, of closely related names like "Aristoteles") going back to an original use in which the name was directly attached to the object by a process of "baptism" of the object with the name. We can speak of Aristotle, the Greek philosopher of long ago, by using the name "Aristotle" because, and only because, this name is connected in the right way to that person, through a historical chain of uses of names all the way back to an original naming or baptism of Aristotle by a name, "Aristoteles," that initiated the historical chain:

> A name "*a*" denotes an object *x* just in case our use of "*a*" is caused by an appropriate chain of uses of "*a*" initiated by a baptism of *x* by "*a*."

A parallel story may be told about the application of a predicate to an object. A predicate "*F*" applies to an object *x* just in case *x* falls into the extension of "*F*." And that happens when *x* belongs to a set of objects covered by "*F*." But *x* belongs to such a set when it is similar (in the right way) to certain other members of the extension of "*F*" that figured in the introduction of "*F*." "A dog" applies to Fido because Fido falls into the extension of the predicate "a dog," and this happens because Fido is similar (in the right way) to members of the extension of "a dog" to which we pointed in introducing the predicate—members baptized using the predicate "a dog." We can call Fido a dog using the predicate "a dog" because Fido is like the entities to which we originally pointed to introduce that predicate. Or, going the other way around, we introduced the predicate "a dog" to cover entities like the ones to which we pointed in originally introducing the predicate. Schematically, the causal theory of application says this:

> A predicate "*F*" applies to an object *x* just in case our use of "*F*" is suitably causally related to *x*.

More fully,

> "*F*" applies to *x* just in case our use of "*F*" is causally related in a certain way to an initial set f' of objects used to baptize the predicate, and there is a set *f* members of which are similar to the members of f', and *x* belongs to *f*

where, speaking informally, the set *f* is the extension of "*F*," and the set f' is the set of members of *f* to which we pointed in originally introducing the predicate "*F*."

Clearly, it is a difficult matter to work out the details of the causal theory of denotation and application. It is difficult to say just what counts as baptism or as an appropriate chain of uses. And there are a host of other matters that would have to be cleared up to make the causal theory fly. But much of this work has already been done for various versions of the causal theory (see, for example, Devitt 1981), and in any case the general idea should be clear. The idea is, roughly, that a chain of uses "transmits" the denotation of the name from the object *x* to our current use of the name "*a*."

I have presented Field's theory as a definition of truth for languages. To develop it for beliefs or propositions, we would either have to understand these as compositional in a language-like way or we would have to assign them truth-conditions indirectly in virtue of their relation to sentences. It is natural enough to treat beliefs as compositional. And something analogous to a causal theory of denotation and application could be worked out for beliefs. But we need not delve into the matter.

Assuming that something like the causal theory of denotation and application is defensible, Field's definition has many advantages over Tarski's conception. It escapes the four drawbacks of Tarski's definition of truth listed a few paragraphs back. It is not limited to defining truth for languages with finitely many names and predicates (since it does not offer a disjunctive definition, as Tarski's conception does). Thus, the theory may define truth for languages with infinitely many names and predicates. The language in which the definition is stated need not contain the language for which truth is defined, as Tarski's definition and the deflationary definition require. Understanding the definition of truth for a language does not require understanding the language. Finally, Field's definition provides the framework for a genuine reduction of truth to physicalist concepts or at least to nonsemantical concepts. These are some of the advantages over Tarski's theory. And of course Field's theory has the advantage over Austin's theory of giving compositional truth-conditions down to the terms and predicates.

The theory does not automatically avoid entailing Bivalence (nor does Austin's), but it can be modified to do so by restricting it to sentences with precise predicates and then adding an account of truth for sentences with vague predicates, such as a supervaluational (Fine 1976) or many-valued (Sanford 1977) account.

The advantages of Field's theory seem great enough to warrant taking it seriously as an account of truth that may serve the explanatory role that motivates the correspondence theory. Is there, then, any objection to the approach that might get in the way of its accomplishing this goal?

Dorothy Grover (1990) has protested that the notion of truth Field defines cannot play the explanatory role that motivates the correspondence theory and indeed that his theory is not even a correspondence theory. Let us consider these objections.

(1) It is said that Field's theory is not a correspondence theory because a correspondence theory would entail that the word-world relations defining truth differ from those defining falsehood. Yet on Field's theory these do not in fact differ. For according to the theory,

> "*a* is *F*" is true just in case "*F*" applies to the object denoted by "*a*."

But

> "*F*" applies to the object denoted by "*a*" just in case there is an object *x* such that our use of "*F*" is suitably causally related to an initial set of objects f', members of *f* are similar (in the right way) to members of f', our use of "*a*" is suitably causally related to *x*, and *x* belongs to *f*.

Falsehood, in contrast, is presumably defined this way:

> "*a* is *F*" is false just in case our use of "*F*" is causally related to f', members of *f* are similar to members of f',

our use of "a" is causally related to x, and x does not belong to f.

The objection is now that on this theory, truth and falsehood involve the *same word-world relations*. The definitions of truth and falsehood *both* require that our use of "F" is causally related to f', members of f are similar to members of f', and our use of "a" is causally related to x. Thus, the definitions of truth and falsehood differ only in whether x belongs to f. But *this is simply a matter of the way the world is*. It has nothing to do with word-world relations. Consequently, Field's theory does not distinguish truth and falsity in the way a correspondence theory would. It distinguishes them in the way a *deflationary* theory would. It makes the difference between truth and falsehood a matter of what is the case, not a matter of any correspondence between words and the world. But then the approach does not offer a correspondence theory. The burden of the difference between truth and falsity is carried entirely by the last clause of the definitions—whether x belongs to f or does not belong to f. Given that the other clauses in the definitions of truth and falsity do no work in explaining the difference between truth and falsity, Field's theory does not differ from a deflationary theory in its explanation of the difference between truth and falsity. Thus, we should reconsider whether a deflationary theory cannot do the work done by Field's theory and do it more simply. So goes the objection.

(2) A closely related objection to Field's theory is that the notion of truth defined by the theory cannot play the explanatory role the notion of truth must play according to the arguments for a correspondence theory. To explain behavior and discharge the other explanatory functions the notion of truth is supposed to play, the word-world relations required for truth must *differ* for true and false sentences. For example, to use T-reliability to explain why some people are successful in

their practices and why others are not successful, we must ascribe T-reliability to some people and ascribe T-unreliability (a high proportion of false beliefs on the topic) to others. To explain, for example, why one cab driver is successful in delivering people to a certain Chicago neighborhood and another is not, we may have to appeal to a difference in the degree of their T-reliability on the location of streets in that neighborhood. But if, as a correspondence theory assumes, truth is a matter of word- (or thought-)world relations, then ascribing T-reliability to some and T-unreliability to others ascribes a difference in the thought-world relations of various beliefs. But on Field's approach, so goes the objection, ascribing T-reliability and ascribing T-unreliability do not ascribe a difference in word-world relations, since the word-world relations do not differ between true and false beliefs. So Field's theory does not furnish a notion of truth that can do what the arguments for the correspondence theory require. It cannot serve in explaining behavior in the way required by the arguments.

How might one defend Field's theory from objection (1), that it falls short of a correspondence theory of truth? It is worth noting, to begin with, that *any* correspondence theory on which the word-world relations are relations of denotation and application will make these relations the same for truth and falsity. This implication of Field's theory is simply a consequence of defining truth in terms of denotation and application and has nothing to do with the particular account of denotation and application, the causal account, Field employs. Since it is hard to see how a compositional truth-definition could avoid defining truth in terms of denotation and application, it seems that any theory of truth on which the notion of truth can perform the explanatory roles attributed by the arguments for the correspondence theory would have the implication of Field's theory. Only a fact or state of affairs correspondence theory could afford different word-world relations for truth and falsity. In other words, no compositional theory could count as a correspondence theory if Field's does not, and thus no correspondence notion of truth could play the explanatory role imposed by the arguments for the correspondence theory. Since these arguments supply the main motive for a correspondence theory, the correspondence theorist has a powerful incentive to find something wrong with the present objection.

The mistake is not far to seek, however. A correspondence theory is simply one that makes truth a relation between words or thoughts and the world. And Field's theory does this. To be sure, on Field's theory, the word-world relations for falsity are the same as those for truth. But that does not mean that the theory is not a correspondence theory or that it distinguishes truth and falsity in the way that a deflationary theory does. On the contrary, the approach reaps a number of benefits by imposing word-world relations in the way it does, even though these are the same for truth and falsity. Most importantly, it can define truth in a metalanguage that does not contain the language for which truth is defined. This enables the correspondence theory to avoid making truth or falsity a relation to the ascriber of truth and falsity. For ascribing truth and falsity does not essentially relate true and false beliefs to the English language. This is the crucial advantage of the correspondence theory over deflationism. For this purpose, it does not matter that the word- (or thought-)world relations are the same for truth and falsity.

These points carry over to objection (2), that on Field's theory the notion of truth cannot do the explanatory work the correspondence notion is supposed to do. The correspondence notion may play its role in the use of the notion of T-reliability to explain successful practices even though truth and falsehood involve the same word-world relations. To be sure, using T-reliability requires a notion of truth for which there are different *conditions* of truth and falsehood. But there is no reason why, for purposes of explaining successful practices, the word-world relations must differ. And so there is no reason why the explanation of successful practices cannot employ the notion of truth Field defines. What is crucial for the motivation for a correspondence theory is that the explanation of successful practices, first, not employ a notion of truth on which our ascribing true beliefs in effect ascribes a relation between subjects and us, the explainers. In other words, a correspondence theory is needed if the notion of truth employed in the explanation does not in effect ascribe a relation between the subject and the explainers. A deflationary notion of truth is ruled out because it has just this feature. The explanation of successful practices must, second, ascribe a relation between words and the world. In this respect, too, the explanation using a correspondence notion of truth differs from an explanation using a deflationary notion. Field's approach meets these two conditions. It thus differs in the required respects from deflationism.

To use T-reliability to explain a person's successful practices, it is necessary to assume that generally the person (mentally) concatenates a name "*a*," a copula "*is*," and a predicate "*F*" to assent to "*a* is *F*" only when "*F*" applies to the object denoted by "*a*" (for a sentence "*a* is *F*" on the relevant topic). Now, on Field's theory, to assume this is in part to assume that the person's use of "*F*" is causally related to special members *f′* of the extension of *f*, and *x* is similar to these members, and the person's use of "*a*" is causally related to object *x*. It is also to assume that the person keeps track of being *F* and object *x* in such a way that he or she concatenates "*a*," "is," and "*F*" so as to believe the proposition expressed by "*a* is *F*" only if *x* is similar to members of *f′*. The use of T-unreliability to explain a person's lack of success in certain practices would make analogous assumptions, except here we would assume that the person fails to keep track of being *F* and object *x* in such a way that he or she concatenates "*a*," "is," and "*F*" so as to believe the proposition expressed by "*a* is *F*" when *x* is not similar to members of *f*′. It is true that assuming the T-reliability or T-unreliability of a subject using a correspondence notion of truth or falsehood does not *by itself* explain why one subject's practices are successful and another's are not. For one thing, the causal relations ascribed in ascribing T-reliability and in ascribing T-unreliability are the same for truth and falsehood. But that does not mean that the explanation is not a correspondence explanation or that it might as well be a deflationary explanation. It cannot be a deflationary explanation if we wish to use T-reliability to explain successful practices, since on a deflationary explanation, ascribing true beliefs is ascribing something about us, the explainers, and the explanation of successful practices can have nothing to do with us.

Now the deflationist could *mimic* the correspondence explanation of successful practices by talking about causal relations in just the way the correspondence explanation does. But then, in explaining these practices the deflationist would no longer be employing a *deflationary* notion of truth. The deflationist might propose dispensing with talk of truth here altogether in favor of talk of the conditions assigned to truth by the correspondence theory.

But that would be a Pyrrhic victory, since it would require the deflationist to give up the claim to define any notion of truth that might be employed here. Moreover, it does not seem that the deflationist can afford to give up this claim. To be sure, the deflationist could replace talk of truth, truth-conditions, content, and T-reliability with talk of causal relations and still be able to offer the same explanations of behavior and successful practices as a correspondentist could offer (though of course doing so would give up the correspondence theory's explanation of the role of truth-conditions in the explanation of behavior and successful practices). Indeed, the correspondence theory *entails* that this replacement will work, since it is one point of the theory to reveal how talk of truth enters into the explanation of behavior by reducing such talk to talk of causal relations. But if in fact we do ascribe truth-conditions in explaining behavior, and the notion of truth employed is the *same* as we employ elsewhere—e.g., in assenting to propositions expressed by sentences we cannot utter—then the correspondence theory characterizes the notion of truth the deflationist attempts to characterize, and the deflationist characterization cannot be right.

These points are enough to defend Field's theory from objections (1) and (2). His theory comes closer than others to doing the job required of a correspondence theory of truth.

III. Nondescriptivist Theories of Truth

My endorsement of the correspondence theory has of course been tentative, contingent not only on the detailed development of the theory, but also on the further exploration of alternative theories. A few parting words about remaining alternatives to the correspondence theory are therefore in order here.

One could skirt my objections to deflationism and the other theories of truth and yet avoid the correspondence theory if one could find a plausible alternative notion of truth on which truth does not involve a relation to a truth-ascriber or to believers. One might propose a *nondescriptivist* view of truth. For example, one might propose an *expressivist* or a *motivational* view of truth. On a nondescriptivist view, talk of truth is not, as the deflationist and the correspondence theorist maintain, talk that, by virtue of meaning, purports to describe the world. On an expressivist view, talk of truth does not describe the world but expresses an attitude. On a motivational view, talk of truth motivates behavior. These views might escape making truth a relation to a truth-ascriber or to believers. Nevertheless, to be plausible, they would have to accommodate the explanatory and expressive powers of the notion of truth cited in our arguments for the correspondence theory.

The only developed nondescriptivist view of truth known to me that does avoid the errors of deflationism and the other views is that of Huw Price (1988, 117-218). On Price's view, the point of truth talk (or at any rate, the point of truth talk incorporated in the meaning of "true" or the nature of truth) is to motivate people to settle their cognitive disagreements by argument.

Price's view has many advantages. It is certain that talk of truth does motivate people to disputation and eventual consensus. In light of this fact, it is natural to explore the suggestion that such a function belongs to the notion of truth by virtue of the meaning of "true." Price's theory avoids entailing that truth involves a deep relation to believers or truth-ascribers. Moreover, Price has shown that his motivational notion of truth mimics a number of other features the notion of truth intuitively has. All this speaks in favor of the motivational view.

However, it is not obvious why we would use, or perhaps even how we *could* use, a motivational notion of truth to ascribe truth conditions for purposes of psychological explanation. What is needed for the psychological explanation of behavior is that the notion of content employed enable us to link the beliefs and desires to the behavior causally. To a rough approximation, the content must be assigned in such a way that the logical or practical-syllogistic relations between the propositional contents mirror the inferential and other causal relations between the beliefs, desires, and behavior. For this purpose, the notion of truth employed in ascribing truth conditions must leave room for logical and practical-syllogistic relations that mirror inferential relations. Indeed, if the use of the notion of truth (rather than some alternative notion) is to be warranted, the notion must make such relations possible.

That the motivational notion will *leave room for* the logical relations may be plausible enough. It is plausible to suppose that disputation will to some degree have to be logical if it is to be persuasive and consensus-inducing—a point made by Peirce. That the motivational notion will make the logical relations *possible* is harder to countenance. Just how a motivational notion could in any sense generate logical relations is obscure. The proponent of the motivational view might offer the proposal that the motivational notion can be used to ascribe contents for purposes of psychological explanation, as long as the logical relations implicitly ascribed in employing the motivational notion are not conceived as part of the *meaning* of "true" or the semantics of the notion of truth (for if they were so conceived, then the notion would no longer be purely motivational but descriptive as well). The trouble with this proposal is that there is no reason to use the motivational notion to ascribe content for purposes of psychological explanation if the logical relations ascribed are not part of the meaning of "true." It is far from obvious, for example, why the contents we ascribe for purposes of psychological explanation should be the same as those we ascribe to propositions to motivate disputation (unless of course the point of disputation can be noncircularly characterized as aiming at true belief—something the motivational theory cannot allow). (Parallel issues arise regarding the practical-syllogistic relations we attribute in psychological explanation. The motivational theory has difficulty explaining the role of the notion of truth in the intentional explanation of action.)

In addition to this, it is hard to see why the motivational notion would afford the expressive powers of the notion of truth. On the contrary, there is no obvious disputation- and consensus-motivating point in ascribing truth to propositions not expressible in our home language.

In sum, there is no obvious reason why Price's motivational notion of truth and our common notion should be the same.

At the very least, Price's view will fail to explain certain features of the notion of truth that are plausibly regarded as part of its semantics. But then the motivational function of the notion of truth does not tell the whole semantical story about the notion. That said, we should recognize that Price's view remains in an early stage of development. The view will need further elaboration before we can pronounce final judgment on it. And of course we must keep our eyes open for other nondescriptivist theories of truth.

In this chapter, I have offered several arguments for a correspondence theory of truth: the arguments from explaining behavior, defining T-reliability, using the notion of T-reliability in inference from testimony and in reliance on others to perform tasks, and the role of the notion of T-reliability in explaining successful practices. All turn on whether truth implicitly involves a relation to a truth-ascriber and thus whether truth in one way has to do with us. Thus, the arguments in favor of the correspondence theory supplement various objections in earlier chapters to pragmatism, coherentism, and deflationism. These objections turned on whether, by its nature or by the meaning of "true," truth depends on the mind or otherwise involves a deep relation to believers or truth-ascribers. The present arguments for the correspondence theory reinforce the mounting evidence of earlier chapters that truth does *not* involve such a deep relation to believers or truth-ascribers. It involves only the shallow relation to believers mentioned in the correspondence theory.

In addition to supplying arguments for the correspondence theory, I have replied to several objections to the theory. I have argued for Field's correspondence theory in preference to Austin's and Moore's. And I have raised preliminary objections to the best developed nondescriptivist theory of truth. We now have before us the outlines of a theory that has some chance of honoring the explanatory work and the expressive power we intuitively ascribe to the notion of truth.

Chapter Seven

Truth and Knowledge

Our knowledge of things is clearly some kind of relation between ourselves and the things known. Truth, by contrast, does not obviously involve an intimate relation between ourselves and other things. Therein lies the source of much contention over truth, since knowledge and truth are evidently closely tied. The pragmatist and the coherentist seize on the apparent contradiction between these claims to argue that truth must after all involve an intimate relation between ourselves and other things. The correspondentist, on the other hand, must deny that knowledge and truth are as intimately tied as they may seem.

I put my money on the correspondentist here. The question before us is whether we should relieve the tension between the three claims above by allowing, with the pragmatist and the coherentist, that truth involves a relation to ourselves, or whether we should instead relieve it by denying a close tie between knowledge and truth. I favor the latter approach. I would like, however, to deal with this issue in the broader setting of the relation between epistemology and the theory of truth. Only by discussing a range of issues regarding the tie between knowledge and truth will we learn the best response to the apparent contradiction that drives pragmatism and coherentism.

One reason, a trivial one, why the nature of knowledge bears on theories of truth is that some knowledge is what we might call *knowledge of truth.* That is, some knowledge is knowledge that has as its content a proposition about truth; it is knowledge *that a proposition is true.* One way to test a theory of truth, then, is by asking whether it is consistent with our having such knowledge of truth. This is the reasoning to be found in the epistemological objections to pragmatism and coherentism. But this is not the only way in which the nature of knowledge may bear on truth. I wish to ask more broadly what the nature of knowledge implies for truth.

The idea I want to judge here is *epistemological autonomism*:

> The nature of knowledge neither rules out nor entails any particular theory of truth.

On this view, a correct account of knowledge neither excludes nor enforces deflationism, the correspondence theory, pragmatism, or coherentism. Now, we have already seen (in Chapters 3 and 4) that epistemological autonomism is not strictly correct: there are forceful *epistemological* objections to pragmatism and coherentism. In other words, a correct account of knowledge *does* rule out certain theories of truth. However, the knowledge in question here is of a *specific* kind—knowledge of truth or knowledge that propositions are true.

I want to ask in this chapter whether epistemological autonomism might nevertheless be substantially correct. Are there any *fully general* features of knowledge—features belonging to *all* knowledge and not just knowledge of truth—that rule out any particular theories of truth? I wish to ask especially whether there are any fully general features of knowledge that favor or rule out the theories of truth I take most seriously, deflationism and the correspondence theory. That is, I wish to look into the plausibility of *epistemological deflationism*, the view that

> The nature of knowledge requires no more than a *deflationary* conception of truth.

According to epistemological deflationism, the nature of knowledge does not require a correspondence notion of truth. (See Williams 1986 and Horwich 1990 for examples of epistemological deflationism, and Friedman 1979 for opposition to the view.) Let us note that epistemological deflationism does not entail epistemological autonomism, since the nature of knowledge might rule out pragmatism and coherentism even if it requires no more than a deflationary conception of truth. I wish to ask about the plausibility of both epistemological deflationism and epistemological autonomism. I also wish to return to the related question, raised in Chapter 1 and subsequently, whether a correspondence theory is committed to skepticism.

I. Truth and the Analysis of Knowledge

A bit of reflection on the role of truth in the analysis of knowledge and justification reveals that there are fully general considerations about knowledge that show that epistemological deflationism is not strictly correct (nor is epistemological autonomism). Plausible theories of knowledge and justification must employ a notion of truth that is more than deflationary.

There are in fact two ways the notion of truth enters into an account of knowledge and justification, and both of these involve a nondeflationary notion of truth.

(1) The notion of truth makes an appearance in the specification of *characteristically epistemic goals*. The point of specifying these goals is to differentiate knowledge and justification,

and more generally epistemic value, from other "modes" of value—from moral, aesthetic, legal, or prudential value. The latter modes of value are defined by their own characteristic goals. Moral value might be defined in terms of human welfare: the morally right actions are the ones that in some way contribute to human welfare. Alternatively, it might be defined formally as overriding or all-things-considered value—whatever value overrides other values. Epistemic value, by contrast, is defined by *epistemic* goals, and one of these goals is, on the usual view, the goal of true belief. The goal of true belief has been variously defined as: believing all and only true propositions, believing all and only important true propositions, believing true propositions in large numbers and high proportion, believing true and informative propositions, or believing *p* just in case $\langle p \rangle$ is true. But we need not plump for one of these alternative definitions of the goal of true belief. Nor should we assume that true belief is the sole epistemic goal; there may be other goals—e.g., informative, coherent, simple, explanatory, or fecund belief. But whether or not there are other goals than true belief, the characterization of the epistemic goal is one important role for the notion of truth. (See BonJour 1985, 5-15, for further discussion.) And as I will argue momentarily, this role is inconsistent with epistemological deflationism and autonomism.

(2) The notion of truth plays another, related role as well. It appears in the conditions of knowledge and justification. For ease of discussion, it will help to work with the widely accepted view that knowledge is justified true belief. Schematically,

A subject *S* knows that *p* just in case
(a) $\langle p \rangle$ is true;
(b) *S* believes *p*; and
(c) *S* is justified in believing *p*.

The notion of truth gets into these conditions in at least two ways.

First, it enters into the conditions of knowledge because, as (a) indicates in the schema above, knowledge entails truth:

S knows that *p* only if <*p*> is true.

This commonplace is nearly uncontroversial among epistemologists, but in my experience students not yet initiated in the subject often balk at the idea. Let me, then, say a word in defense of the claim.

Reflect on the absurdity of the remark "Rita knows that she put the umbrella in her car, but it is not true that she did." The absurdity of this utterance is most straightforwardly explained if the first part of the statement is taken to contradict the second. But if there is a contradiction here, then knowledge entails truth. For the first point contradicts the second only if the first point entails that it *is* true that Rita put the umbrella in her car. Another example that leads to the same conclusion is the joke made by Will Rogers: "It isn't what he doesn't know that worries me. It's what he knows that just ain't so." The humor here derives from the absurdity of this remark, which seems to lie in the logical impossibility of someone knowing something that isn't so—isn't true.

Now, it might be offered as evidence against the claim that knowledge entails truth that we say things like "The medievals knew the earth is flat," even though it is false that the earth is flat. This example carries little weight, however. For we can reconcile this kind of talk with the claim that knowledge entails truth by putting "know" in scare quotes. The statement is a misleading way of saying that the medievals *all but knew* that the earth is flat—or that it was *as if* they knew this. In other words, the medieval belief that the earth is flat satisfied all the conditions of knowledge but truth. Treating the flat earth example this way would make it parallel to the natural interpretation of similar statements about perception. For example, we reconcile the truth of the statement "He sees pink elephants" with the fact that seeing entails believing by putting "sees" in scare quotes. What we mean is that it is *as if* he were seeing pink elephants. Nor will it work to go the opposite route and put scare quotes on "know" in our first two examples, saying that the scare quote "know" entails truth but the ordinary "know" does not. For putting "know" in scare quotes in the first two examples would leave us without any way of explaining the impropriety of the statements. Indeed, it would rob the statements of their absurdity. So if scare quotes are to be used to reconcile all these examples, they will have to be placed on the word "know" in the flat earth example. The upshot is that we should maintain the commonplace view that knowledge entails truth.

The notion of truth may also appear in the conditions of knowledge and justification, other than the condition of truth. For example, according to *reliabilism* about justification, a view mentioned in Chapter 4,

> *S* is justified in believing *p* only if *S*'s belief that *p* results from a reliable belief-forming process—a process that tends to yield true beliefs.

Here the notion of truth figures in the conditions of justification even if justification does not entail truth. (See Goldman 1986 and Schmitt 1992 for development of reliabilism.)

Now how do these roles of the notion of truth in the characterization of the epistemic goals and in the conditions of knowledge and justification bear on epistemological deflationism and autonomism? It might at first seem that epistemological deflationism is easily vindicated for these conditions. In the case of the characteristic epistemic goals, it seems that we can speak of the goal of believing a proposition *p* just in case *p*, rather than the goal of believing *p* just in case <*p*> is true.

So talk of truth drops out of the picture. Similarly, in the case of the conditions of knowledge, it might seem that the conditions can easily dispense with talk of truth entirely without loss of content. Thus, we may replace the conditions above with:

> *S* knows that *p* only if *p*.

And

> *S* is justified in believing *p* only if *S*'s belief that *p* results from a process that is reliable in the sense that, for most propositions <*p*>, if the process yields the belief that *p*, then *p*.

Neither of these conditions employs the notion of truth.

Does this vindicate epistemological deflationism? In fact, these plausible-looking attempts at replacement flop. The strategy here runs into the same trouble as the attempt to deflate truth in such claims as "Whatever God believes is true"—a problem we discussed in Chapter 5. Consider, for example, the claim "God knows more propositions than we can express in English." This claim does not appear to be self-contradictory. Yet ascribing deflationary truth-conditions to the content of the knowledge that we attribute to God would make it so. For example, dressing the claim with *substitutional* quantification over propositions would make it equivalent to "There are propositions expressible in English such that God knows them, but these propositions are not expressible in English." But of course the latter claim is a contradiction. Similarly, we might want to say "People can be justified in believing things not expressible in English." Yet on reliabilism, under a deflationary theory of truth (and under one other plausible assumption we need not go into here), this claim will be self-contradictory. So epistemological deflationism is incorrect. The notion of truth employed here is not merely deflationary. Epistemological deflationism and autonomism fail.

Nevertheless, despite this failure, the question remains how badly these views fail. Deflationism is ruled out by the role of the notion of truth in epistemology. And pragmatism and coherentism may be ruled out too (for the reasons given in Chapters 3 and 4). Does the epistemological role of the notion of truth further constrain the nature of truth?

At least one nondeflationary theory of truth (or class of theories) is ruled out by plausible theories of knowledge and justification—namely, *epistemic* theories of truth like the coherence and superjustification theories from Chapter 4. Epistemic theories of truth are ruled out on pain of circularity. For these theories define truth in terms of justification. But plausible theories of justification define justification in terms of the epistemic goal of true belief. Consequently, epistemic theories of truth are circular. In my view, this makes a serious objection to the theories, an objection additional to the epistemological objection discussed in Chapter 4.

Hilary Putnam (1983) has noted the inconsistency between epistemic theories of truth and "veritistic" theories of justification (i.e., theories of justification, such as reliabilism, that define justification in terms of truth). However, Putnam draws the opposite conclusion from the one I draw: veritistic theories of justification must be repudiated because they conflict with epistemic theories of truth.

How should we react to the inconsistency between epistemic theories of truth and veritistic theories of justification? One apparently reconciling point is that some theories of truth that appear to be epistemic really define truth not in terms of justification but in other terms. The coherence theory of truth, for example, defines truth in terms of coherence. Such a theory is not ruled out on grounds of circularity alone. There is, however, an additional objection to these theories that does rule them out. This is an objection that decides in favor of veritistic theories of justification and against epistemic and like-minded theories of truth. Our objection here is more general than the objections to specific epistemic theories like the superjustification theory.

To see the objection, it will help to consider a version of epistemological deflationism more radical than any we have so far considered. This is a version that bears some resemblance to epistemic theories of truth but rejects the idea that truth is itself an epistemic notion.

Radical epistemological deflationism admits that the notions of knowledge and justification, as traditionally conceived, are characterized in terms of a nondeflationary notion of truth but insists at the same time that we do not need such notions. According to this view, we can make do with a notion of justified belief (or warranted assertibility, as it is sometimes called) that is not characterized in terms of truth, appending to it at most a deflationary notion of truth. The point here is not Putnam's point that we cannot have a veritistic theory of justification because truth is an epistemic notion. It is rather that we do not need a veritistic notion of justification because a nonveritistic notion is available, and we do not need a nondeflationary notion of truth because the nonveritistic notion of justification can do all the work we need done. This view leaves its proponents free to embrace whatever notion of truth they wish—though it would be most natural to embrace a deflationary notion of truth. Richard Rorty (1982, 1991) has made remarks that suggest a view like this, though other remarks he has made suggest contrary views, and I will not attempt the ticklish task of interpreting him. It is worth noting that the radical epistemological deflationism on offer here bears some resemblance to the pragmatist view, scouted in Chapter 3, that the notion of truth is useless because it does not conform to a pragmatic theory of meaning. John Dewey's remarks about truth and warrant sometimes intimate such a view.

How might radical epistemological deflationism be supported? It might be said in its favor that justified belief may be characterized by certain rules governing our practices in forming beliefs and reflecting our practices in evaluating beliefs. These rules would take a form telling us which propositions to believe, given what we already believe and given our experiences and circumstances. It might be said that these rules govern our belief-forming practices because they reflect our evaluative practices. The rules need not themselves employ the concept of truth, and the justification they characterize need not be in any sense directed toward true belief. If this is so, then there is a way of characterizing justified belief that does not employ the concept of truth. It must be admitted, however, that the characterization will still forbid us from saying all that we want to be able to say, unless we append to it a correspondence theory of truth; for if the truth-conditions ascribed to beliefs are deflationary, they severely limit our powers of expression and explanation. But proponents of the present view tend to have sailed far enough from customary intellectual life to be willing to live with the expressive and explanatory limitations of their view, in exchange for the convenience of doing without a correspondence theory of truth. The view enables one to characterize justification without commitment to any particular theory of truth.

The question remains, however, whether the notion of justified belief can do all the work we want done without appending a nondeflationary notion of truth. It might be—and has been—claimed that the only function of the notion of truth that cannot be performed either by a deflationary notion of truth or by the notion of justified belief is the "cautionary" function of the notion of truth—its use in such utterances as

> I'm justified in believing *p*, but of course my belief might not be true.

"True" here cannot be taken to mean "justified," since that would make the utterance a contradiction. (The claim that this is the only function of the notion of truth that cannot be performed either by a deflationary notion or by the notion of justified belief is of course mistaken if the explanatory arguments for the correspondence theory are good. But I will waive this observation for the time being.)

At this point, the proponent of radical epistemological deflationism may say that even though in its cautionary use "true" does not mean "justified," it gets whatever content it may have from the contrast between what I am currently justified in believing and what I would later be justified in believing were I to carry on in an epistemically optimal manner (i.e., according to the rules of justification). I can only think that I might be justified in believing *p* even though *p* is not true because I can see how I might later cease to be justified in believing *p*.

There are several objections to radical epistemological deflationism. One is that the notion of justified belief cannot do all the epistemological work the notion of truth does. In particular, it cannot supply whatever content the notion of truth may have in utterances like the one above (i.e., "I'm justified in believing *p*, but of course my belief might not be true"). To begin with, in making that utterance, I am not holding up my own future justified belief as a standard against which to judge my current justified belief. For I could equally well say

> I am justified in believing *p*, but even if I continued to be so justified after further inquiry, my belief might still be false.

At this point the radical epistemological deflationist might deny that the standard of truth can have any content here. If our best effort at belief could not overturn the belief that *p*, then, it might be said, there can be no point in holding up a possibly contrary standard. For we could never justifiedly employ that standard to revise our beliefs. To put the radical epistemological deflationist's contention succinctly, there can be no practical use of "true" of the cautionary sort I am describing. And if there is no practical use, then there is no contentful use.

One thing to notice about this contention is its dependence on a pragmatic theory of meaning: "true" can have no content beyond the cautionary use if it has no *practical* use of the cautionary sort I am describing. We have, however, seen reasons for rejecting the pragmatic theory of meaning. But even waiving the plausibility of the pragmatic theory of meaning, there is a difficulty with the radical epistemological deflationist's contention. It is true that we could never justifiedly employ a standard of truth of the sort just described. But there may yet be a practical point to the cautionary use of "true" of the sort I am describing, even if we cannot employ it as a standard to revise our beliefs. One point that the cautionary use might have is to supply a rationale for our rules of justification: our rules aim at true belief. In recognizing that our belief may fall short of truth, we need not be proposing a standard for revising our beliefs but merely reminding ourselves that our rules are *aimed* at true belief. The only rules we count as rules of justification are those that contribute to this aim.

Of course, the radical epistemological deflationist will deny the need for such a rationale or reminder: the rules of justification are simply those which actually govern our belief-forming practice and codify our evaluative practice; they need no rationale; and the beliefs we count as true are simply those sanctioned by the rules. The radical epistemological deflationist will say that our objection gets the relation between truth and justification backwards: true belief is the upshot, not the rationale, of justification.

I am inclined to regard this as unsatisfactory. If nothing more can be said about why certain rules are rules of justification than that they codify our evaluative practice, then we can supply no serious reason why certain rules are rules of justification, rules to be obeyed in forming beliefs, while other rules are not rules of justification. We can only say that we evaluate things this way. Yet we surely think that we can give a serious reason. Indeed, it is part of our evaluative practice to give such reasons for counting rules as rules of justification. The rationale for counting a rule a rule of justification is that the rule contributes to the aim of true belief. Of course if our evaluative practice requires us to give such a reason, then, plausibly, there is a distinct rule—a metarule of justification, if you like—governing the metapractice of giving such reasons. But that hardly changes the fact that there is a metapractice of giving reasons for counting rules as rules of justification, and that the notion of truth involved in this metapractice does not get its content from any notion of future justification.

The cautionary use of "true" has another and related point: to supply a rationale for the metapractice of revising the rules of justification (see Okrent 1993 for a similar view). If we are to revise our rules of justification as well as our beliefs, we need some standard by which to revise these rules. But that standard does seem to need a rationale external to the rules of justification themselves. In particular, it needs a rationale in *the aim of true belief*.

To see this, let us ask whether the rules of justification could police themselves. Ostensibly, we would revise a rule when it conflicts with other rules (or, in a case that raises parallel issues, with beliefs that conform to other rules). Rules conflict when they jointly entail inconsistent evaluations of beliefs—i.e., when they jointly entail that some belief is both justified and unjustified. When rules conflict in this way, some rule must be jettisoned. Presumably, though, there must be a reason for keeping some rules rather than others. The need for a notion of truth arises when we consider this reason. It is clear that the basis for rule revision cannot be supplied by the rules themselves. The basis must be external to the rules. At the same time, it is hard to see how the reason given could avoid employing the notion of truth.

Consider, for example, this basis for revision: revise rules so as to maximize the *content* of the beliefs sanctioned by the rules. This is a plausible enough basis and one to which proponents of a coherence theory of justification or rule revision might be inclined to subscribe. It is also one to which the radical epistemological deflationist might be attracted. But this basis employs the notion of content. Hence, it employs the notion of truth-conditions, if the notion of content is nonprojectivist. Note, further, that the notion of content must be nonprojectivist if the rules of justification determine the meanings of words, as radical epistemological deflationists tend to hold. For if the rules of justification determine the meanings of words, then a revision of the rules will change these meanings, and it will be impossible for us to assign content across such a change merely by relying on our own language. In other words, if there is a change of meaning across a revision of the rules, as radical epistemological deflationists tend to hold, then the content assigned to beliefs after the revision cannot be *our* content before the revision; hence it cannot be projectivist content. A nonprojectivist view of content—hence a notion of truth not available to the radical epistemological deflationist—is needed.

Of course we have so far looked at only one example of a basis for revising the rules of justification—maximize the content of the beliefs sanctioned by the rules. There might be other bases. But I would make two remarks about this. One remark is that, whatever basis for revising the rules may be found, it is apt to at least *include* considerations about maximizing the content of beliefs. In this case, there will be no escaping the need for a notion of truth in the basis for revision. The other remark is that further considerations are apt to include, among other things, a preference for *avoiding inconsis-*

tent beliefs. And the most persuasive reason for avoiding inconsistent beliefs is that the rules of justification aim at true belief. It might be thought that there is an alternative reason to avoid inconsistent beliefs: inconsistent beliefs, it might be said, commit one to believing just any proposition, since they entail all propositions. One might prefer to avoid inconsistent beliefs in order to avoid commitment to believing just any proposition. But this is not obviously independent of the preference for true beliefs. For the best reason to avoid commitment to believing just any proposition is to avoid a *false* belief. Here again the notion of truth cannot be understood in terms of future justification, since it enters into the characterization of justification. It seems, then, that the reason for revising the rules of justification as we do must employ a notion of truth whose content cannot be given merely by future justification.

At this point, the radical epistemological deflationist might insist that there are *metarules* that decide between conflicting rules of justification, and these metarules govern the revision of the rules without employing the notion of truth. I am inclined to grant that there are metarules that decide between conflicting rules, and that these metarules could be formulated without employing the notion of truth. But such a formulation would divest the rules of the rationale that we so evidently supply for them and without which they make no sense.

We might put our overall point here by saying that, so long as we restrict our attention to the rules of justification that govern belief-formation, we may not feel the need for the rationale of aiming at true belief. But once we turn to the metarules that govern rule revision, we can no longer ignore the role that the aim of true belief plays in the system of epistemic norms. In short, the notion of truth does play a role in the epistemic system, and this notion cannot get its content from the notion of future justification. Epistemology needs a notion of truth not understood in this way. For this reason, as well as the others we marshalled in Chapter 4, we must reject an epistemic notion of truth. And we must also reject radical epistemological deflationism.

Let us recall, finally, our conclusion in Chapter 6 that a nondeflationary notion of truth is needed for explanatory and expressive purposes. Despite what the radical epistemological deflationist assumes, we would need a nondeflationary notion of truth even if epistemological purposes did not require it. This version of deflationism gains what plausibility it has from emphasizing the epistemological function of the notion of truth to the exclusion of its explanatory function.

The upshot for epistemological deflationism and autonomism is that these views are mistaken at least to this extent: the characterization of knowledge and justified belief requires a nondeflationary notion of truth, and epistemic theories of truth are ruled out on grounds of circularity because the notion of truth plays a deep role in the system of epistemic norms. For the same reason, however, we must resist going as far as the radical epistemological deflationist claim that the notion of justified belief requires no nondeflationary notion of truth.

II. Truth and Skepticism

Is there any further case against epistemological autonomism? Does the view also fail because the correspondence theory of truth is ruled out on epistemological grounds? We have in the course of this book seen many epistemological arguments for idealism, relativism, the coherence theory, and the pragmatic theory of truth, as well as epistemological objections to the coherence and pragmatic theories. We have not, however, given due attention to the core of these arguments—the epistemological argument against the correspondence theory of truth. It is time to redress that omission. The result will bear directly on the plausibility of epistemological autonomism.

The complaint against the correspondence theory, once again, is that it denies that truth involves a relation to us. Yet knowledge and truth are intimately related, and knowledge involves a relation to us. I will focus on the version of this complaint that is historically most important.

According to this version, a realist correspondence theory gives rise to *Cartesian skepticism* (B. Williams 1978, 32-71, Stroud 1984, 1-38). We may take Cartesian skepticism to be the view that we have no knowledge because we might be deceived by a demon into believing what we do even though our beliefs are false. The Cartesian skeptic alleges that, for all we know, it might be that our experiences are produced in us, not by physical bodies, but by a demon bent on making it seem as if our experiences are produced by physical bodies. We lack knowledge because we have no way of ruling out this horrific possibility.

The charge against the correspondence theory is that Cartesian skepticism is inevitable once we accept a realist correspondence theory of truth. For such a theory prevents us from ruling out systematic deception of the sort imposed by the demon. Thus, it is said, a realist correspondence theory of truth generates Cartesian skepticism. We may avoid Cartesian skepticism only by forswearing a realist correspondence theory. Avoiding skepticism, or so the argument goes, requires embracing an idealist metaphysics or a noncorrespondence theory of truth.

Now why is a realist correspondence theory supposed to give rise to skepticism? In outline, the argument is that on a realist correspondence theory, truth is a relation to an independently existing world. But once truth is held distinct from thought in this way, we have lost any prospect of the kind of epistemic access to the world necessary for knowledge. Consequently, we lack knowledge. There is nothing we can do to rule out the possibility that our beliefs are systematically false.

To review the matter more closely, according to the standard argument for Cartesian skepticism, knowledge requires epistemic access to the truth. In particular, it requires us to rule out the possibility of error. But on a realist correspondence theory, truth is a relation to a mind-independent world. So knowledge requires epistemic access to a mind-independent world. But no such epistemic access is possible. For we are unable to rule out the possibility of error about a mind-independent world. Because the world is independent of our minds, there is no forestalling the possibility that we are radically mistaken in our beliefs about it. To avoid Cartesian skepticism, then, we must reject a realist correspondence theory.

Is it true, as this line of reasoning would have us believe, that the only way to avoid Cartesian skepticism is to reject a realist correspondence theory? Let us begin our evaluation of the reasoning by noting that there are several premises in the skeptical argument. The realist correspondence theory is only one premise. And it might turn out that other premises are less plausible—hence should be rejected before we reject the realist correspondence theory.

Indeed, it seems on inspection that one other premise is at least as vulnerable as the realist correspondence theory. This is the premise that knowledge requires epistemic access to the truth. This premise would seem to be at least as vulnerable as the realist correspondence theory. To judge whether we may deny this premise rather than the realist correspondence theory, we must have a better idea than we have yet gotten of what epistemic access is. Of course if "epistemic access" is given a weak enough reading, the premise that knowledge requires epistemic access will be shellproof. It will be so, if, for example, epistemic access is said to be nothing other than knowledge. In this case, the premise will be trivially true. But by the same token, the premise will not entail a requirement of access that prohibits knowledge of a mind-independent reality.

In other words, if the premise is interpreted in this way, the skeptical argument will simply fall flat—in which case it poses no threat to a realist correspondence theory.

The argument for skepticism, in short, needs a stronger reading of the premise that knowledge requires epistemic access. Let us begin with one stronger reading that promises a skeptical conclusion. It will be convenient to take this reading as a sample interpretation of the premise before making more general remarks about the prospects for a requirement of epistemic access that can generate skepticism.

What is required for epistemic access, on this stronger reading, is the ability to *deduce* the proposition known from one's *mental representations' having the content they do*. On this reading, epistemic access to, say, the proposition that this is an elm requires that the subject deduce this proposition from the proposition that he or she has a certain experience (e.g., an experience of this seeming to be an elm). Call this interpretation of the requirement of epistemic access the *deduction from experience* interpretation.

The reason for such a strong requirement would be this. It is plausible that the subject has epistemic access to the contents of his or her experience. For the subject cannot be deceived by a demon into thinking that he or she has a certain experience with a certain content—e.g., that it seems to the subject that this is an elm—unless the subject *does* have that experience (i.e., it *does* seem to the subject that this is an elm). There is no way for the subject to be deceived about the content of experience. Thus, if the subject can deduce a proposition from having an experience with a certain content, then the subject cannot be deceived about that proposition either. This must be enough for epistemic access, since all that epistemic access requires is a guarantee that the subject is not deceived. So deduction from experience is enough for epistemic access.

Now, on the deduction from experience interpretation of epistemic access, skepticism does follow from the premise that knowledge requires epistemic access. Unless the proposition that this is an elm can be *analyzed* in terms of propositions about the contents of mental representations (e.g., that it seems to the subject that this is an elm), it will not be possible to deduce the proposition that this is an elm from experience in the manner required by the deduction from experience interpretation of epistemic access. That is, unless *phenomenalism* is correct, we will not have epistemic access to the proposition that this is an elm (see Chapter 1 for discussion of phenomenalism and its foibles). And so we will not know this proposition. So if we assume a form of realism inconsistent with phenomenalism, then skepticism follows on the present interpretation of epistemic access. We can save ourselves from skepticism only by accepting a particular version of idealism—phenomenalism.

How should we react to the discovery that the premise that knowledge requires epistemic access, on the deduction from experience interpretation, leads to skepticism, given a realist correspondence theory? As I have indicated, the argument is taken to show that if we wish to avoid skepticism, we must abandon the realist correspondence theory. Is this what we should do?

As a preliminary step in judging whether this is the right reaction, we should note that the only role a realist correspondence theory of truth plays in the argument for skepticism is to rule out phenomenalism. In other words, no work is done by the correspondence theory itself, only by a certain kind of realism—the kind inconsistent with phenomenalism. In fact, realism here is merely the denial of phenomenalism. Thus, the most the argument could show is that if we wish to avoid skepticism, we should reject such realism, not the correspondence theory.

But the argument does not really show even this much. For its only leverage against realism is that applied by the assumption of phenomenalism. To show that we should abandon realism, the argument must assume phenomenalism. But since realism—the denial of phenomenalism—is far more plausible than phenomenalism (for the reasons given in Chapter 1), the argument has no force. In other words, we must react to the argument, not by abandoning realism, but by rejecting the premise that knowledge requires epistemic access on the deduction from experience interpretation.

It remains to ask whether there is any interpretation of epistemic access weaker than the deduction from experience interpretation (which is, admittedly, a very strong interpretation of epistemic access). Is there an interpretation of epistemic access that is weaker and more plausible than the deduction from experience interpretation, and yet at the same time enables one to deduce skepticism from a realist correspondence theory? If there is such an interpretation, then avoiding skepticism may yet drive us to abandon a realist correspondence theory of truth. If not, then we should reject the requirement of epistemic access.

Rather than look at further specific interpretations of epistemic access, I will simply state the requirement of epistemic access in its most general form—or rather, in the most general form it can take and still give rise to Cartesian skepticism (see Schmitt 1992 for further discussion of these issues).

A fully general principle of epistemic access says this:

> Knowledge that *p* requires ruling out the prima facie possibility of a demon who deceives one into believing that *p* when <*p*> is in fact false.

Epistemic access, in other words, demands that one meet all challenges to the truth of one's beliefs. These challenges advert to possibilities one has not yet ruled out—what I will call *prima facie possibilities*. One of these prima facie possibilities has been taken (by Descartes, among others) to have a kind of precedence over the others: the possibility of deception by a demon.

This possibility has been assumed more sweeping than other possibilities in challenging the largest number of beliefs. Indeed ruling out the possibility of deception by a demon is supposed to put one in a position to answer other challenges (such as the possibility that one is merely dreaming what one takes to be real).

On this understanding of the argument for skepticism, the argument runs this way:

(1) It is prima facie possible that we are deceived by a demon.
(2) We can know *p* only if we can rule out the prima facie possibility that we are deceived by a demon into believing *p*.
(3) We cannot rule out this prima facie possibility.
(4) Consequently, we know nothing.

This is a quite general form of the skeptical argument.

The realist correspondence theory of truth is supposed to play a role in supporting premise (1), and epistemic access is identical with premise (2). Premise (3) seems quite right—there is nothing we can do to establish that we are not deceived by a demon. So if we wish to avoid skepticism, we must either reject epistemic access or the realist correspondence theory of truth. It *seems* that we may do either.

It seems so, but on further inspection, the appearance turns out to be misleading. For rejecting the realist correspondence theory of truth will not really help to avoid skepticism here. The only way to avoid skepticism is to reject epistemic access.

To see this, we need only note that premise (1) of the argument for skepticism does not in fact assume a realist correspondence theory of truth. It is true that if we forsake realism for idealism, then we may conclude that it is *not* possible that we are deceived by a demon. For if idealism holds, then we cannot be mistaken about the world—at least, not in the way that we can be if realism holds. And this means that we cannot be deceived by a demon. Many have been tempted to infer from this that premise (1) is mistaken and hence the argument for skepticism falls through. But this temptation should be checked. It is based on a misunderstanding of the import of premise (1). What idealism entails is that it is *metaphysically* impossible for us to be deceived by a demon. That is, it is a genuine ontological impossibility for us to be deceived. This is an impossibility determined by the way things are. But premise (1) does not say that it is *metaphysically* possible for us to be deceived. Rather, it says only that it is *prima facie* possible for us to be deceived. This is not a possibility determined by the way things are, but only by what we know. It means that for all we know, we are deceived by a demon. To say this is not to say that it is actually metaphysically possible for us to be deceived. In general, metaphysical and prima facie possibility are different matters. For Descartes, the demon is metaphysically impossible but, at the outset of the skeptical inquiry, prima facie possible. One cannot infer from the fact that it is metaphysically impossible for us to be deceived, that this is prima facie impossible.

Thus, rejecting realism in favor of idealism will do no damage to premise (1) of the skeptical argument. Now, it is true that if we were entitled to assume idealism at the outset of the skeptical inquiry, then we could use it to reject the metaphysical possibility of deception before the skeptical inquiry got under way. If it were permissible to rely on what we know before entering the skeptical fray, we could then deny premise (1). But surely the skeptic will not allow us to rely at the outset of the skeptical inquiry on any theoretical claims that are themselves brought into doubt by adverting to the prima facie possibility of a deceiving demon. And idealism is such a claim. What counts as a prima facie possibility is determined by our situation at the outset of our joust with the skeptic, and at that point we are entitled only to what the skeptic allows us to bring with us. Idealism is brought into doubt along with other theoretical knowledge.

The idealist might protest that we ought to be able to invoke metaphysical theories for which we have justification to judge whether it is prima facie possible that we are deceived by a demon. But in reply I would note first that even if we were entitled to assume metaphysical theories to answer the skeptic, the idealist could defeat the argument for skepticism only if there were grounds for denying a realist correspondence theory of truth independent of the point that denying this view undermines the argument for Cartesian skepticism. For the strategy now in dispute requires that deception by a demon must be shown *metaphysically* impossible, not prima facie impossible. Yet we have seen no good independent ground for idealism.

But more important, we are not entitled to idealism prior to answering skepticism. We are entitled only to whatever methods and premises escape the prima facie doubts raised by the skeptic, and these methods and premises do not include enough metaphysics to reject the prima facie possibility of a deceiving demon. If we were entitled to assume metaphysical theories, then there would be nothing to stop us from assuming any other claims we have reason to believe. But of course, if we were entitled to assume all of these, the requirement that we be able to rule out the prima facie possibility that we are deceived by a demon would have no force at all. We could argue for any claim for which we have reason. The skeptical argument would trivially lack force. Of course it might be replied that we are not entitled to just any claims we have reason to believe. Rather, we are entitled only to those that we have *a priori* reason to believe. And metaphysical theories fall among the latter claims. But, as Descartes insisted, the prima facie possibility of deception by a demon casts doubt on a priori claims—even simple arithmetical claims like "2 + 2 = 4"—as well as empirical ones. So the fact that metaphysical theories are a priori claims does not secure our entitlement to them in answering the skeptic. We are not entitled to assume idealism in answering skepticism. Idealism does not speak to premise (1).

The idealist might respond by agreeing that embracing idealism and rejecting realism will not avail if our aim is to defeat the skeptical argument by *showing* that a deceiving demon is impossible. For what must be shown is that a deceiving demon is *prima facie* impossible, not that it is merely metaphysically impossible. The claim that a deceiving demon is prima facie possible is an epistemological, not a metaphysical claim, and it is does not entail the metaphysical thesis of a realist correspondence theory. So denying a realist correspondence theory cannot overturn the claim. But one might maintain that even though we cannot show that a deceiving demon is impossible by rejecting realism, we can nevertheless *diagnose what is wrong* with the argument for skepticism by pointing out that a deceiving demon is metaphysically possible only on a realist correspondence theory of truth.

I do not, however, see how this can be correct either. To point out that a deceiving demon is metaphysically possible only on a realist correspondence theory is not to show that there is anything wrong with the argument for skepticism. That would follow only if there were something wrong with including a metaphysical possibility that depends on a realist correspondence theory in the list of prima facie possibilities that generate skeptical doubts at the outset of our joust with the skeptic. And nothing that has been said so far shows that there is anything wrong with including such a metaphysical possibility. Indeed, all that has been said is that we should reject the metaphysical claim of a realist correspondence theory of truth. Yet no *metaphysical* claim can show that there is anything wrong with including a given possibility among the prima facie possibilities. For including a possibility among prima facie possibilities is an epistemological, not a metaphysical position. It is a position on the conduct of our joust with the skeptic. It seems, then, that denying a realist correspondence theory will not suffice to defeat the argument for skepticism.

This being so, the obvious place to look to defeat the argument is premise (2) and epistemic access. In my view, that premise is the one we ought to deny. And it is the one many post-Cartesian theories of knowledge do deny, starting with Spinoza's (1985). Rejecting skepticism is thus consistent with a realist correspondence theory of truth.

What this shows is that the plausibility of a realist correspondence theory is independent of the plausibility of Cartesian skepticism. It is not possible to make the case here, but the points against using the threat of skepticism to overturn a realist correspondence theory provide partial support for a broader conclusion that I regard as true, that there is no persuasive epistemological objection to a realist correspondence theory. That conclusion is supported further by the points made in earlier chapters against the epistemological arguments for idealism, pragmatism, and the coherence theory of truth, as well as by the epistemological objections to the latter two views. I do not believe that epistemology can be used to show that truth in some way turns on a relation to us or to the truth-ascriber.

Thus, we do not have any further case here against epistemological deflationism and autonomism. Though these views are incorrect, we should not exaggerate the relation between metaphysics and epistemology in the way many opponents of a realist correspondence theory do. Epistemological deflationism and autonomism still hint at an important truth. Antipathy to skepticism cannot supply a reason to prefer one theory of truth to another.

In this chapter, we have considered the case against epistemological deflationism and autonomism. Epistemological deflationism is the view that the nature of knowledge requires no more than a deflationary notion of truth. Epistemological autonomism holds that the nature of knowledge neither rules out nor entails any special theory of truth. In earlier chapters, we had already seen that there are challenging epistemological objections to pragmatism and coherentism. This shows that the role of truth in knowledge rules out certain theories of truth, contrary to epistemological autonomism. I have argued here that epistemological deflationism is mistaken, since there are certain things we want to be able to say about knowledge and justification that would be ruled out by a deflationary notion of truth. I have also argued that epistemic theories of truth and radical epistemological deflationism are mistaken because there is a role in epistemic evaluation for a notion of truth that does not get its content from any notion of justification. I have, however, resisted further erosion of epistemological deflationism and autonomism. I have denied that a realist correspondence theory is saddled with skepticism, as often supposed. One cannot infer from the fact that knowledge and truth are intimately related, and that knowledge involves a relation to us, that truth also involves a relation to us. The epistemological deflationist and autonomist are on the money at least to this extent. But in the end, the relations between knowledge and truth are less direct and more complex than either epistemological deflationists and autonomists or their traditionalist opponents have assumed.

Conclusion

The central point of contention in the theory of truth is whether truth involves a relation to thinkers. All theories agree that in *some* sense truth *does* involve such a relation. On the correspondence theory, for example, truth involves a relation between the bearer of truth-values (usually, a sentence, statement, or proposition) and the world (or facts, or objects and their properties), and this relation in turn entails a relation to thinkers. Other theories of truth, however, insist that truth involves a deeper relation to thinkers. According to epistemic theories of truth, truth depends on the mind. According to relativism, pragmatism, and coherentism, truth involves one or another deep relation to thinkers—a relativity to thinkers, a dependence on what it is useful to believe, or a coherence with what the thinker believes. Finally, on deflationism, truth involves a relation to the truth-ascriber. I have sided with the correspondence theorist against these contentions. Truth involves only the relation to thinkers entailed by the correspondence theory. It is a relation between propositions or other truth-bearers and the objects and properties that the constituents of these truth-bearers denote or express.

Recently, there has been much talk in academic circles about, and against, truth. This talk spans quite a few disciplines, including literary theory, anthropology, history, sociology, and speech communication. It has roots in the sociology of science, structuralist linguistics, and feminist theory and arises from some types of historicist and constructivist thinking. One hears protests against classical theories of truth, especially the correspondence theory. And one also hears declamations against the very aim of true belief. These protests by and large turn on whether truth involves some relation to thinkers.

One style of complaint is this: on the correspondence theory, truth does not involve such a relation; but in reality truth does involve such a relation; so the correspondence theory should be rejected. In arguing for the correspondence theory, we have already addressed this complaint; for we have argued that truth does not involve such a relation. Turning then to a second style of complaint, it is said that the correspondence theory is quite right to deny that truth involves a relation to us; but for this very reason, true belief is either unattainable or undesirable, and we should reject the aim of true belief.[1] We have also answered this complaint, since we have defended the correspondence theory from the charge that it makes knowledge and reference impossible.

Though we have answered these complaints against classical theories of truth and the aim of true belief, it remains to address one important worry that motivates these complaints. The worry is that there are diverse cognitive perspectives, perspectives that arise from the diverse cultural, social, political, and economic conditions in which people live. The latter conditions determine, by and large, what people think. Cognitive perspectives, in turn, reinforce and maintain these conditions, helping to ensure the kind of stratification, domination, and oppression that characterizes relations between cultures throughout human history. There is, however, disagreement across cognitive perspectives. The correspondence notion of truth, according to this worry, is central to the suppression of disagreement—and the consequent denigration of cognitive perspectives—that makes cultural domination and oppression possible. The notion of truth, conceived as absolute and as correspondence to reality, has been employed precisely to maintain the stratification and domination of cultures. A dominant culture claims possession of the absolute truth and thus cognitive superiority over another culture. This cognitive superiority is then used to found and justify cultural, social, political, and economic domination. The correspondence notion of truth is thus a tool of cultural and politico-economic domination, and it must be rejected.

I find domination and oppression as appalling as the next person does, and I agree that if the notion of truth were nothing but a weapon of domination of the kind envisaged here, we would be obliged to retire it. But if the argument of Chapter 6 is anywhere near cogent, the notion of truth serves quite different and apparently indispensable explanatory business.

Nor is it clear that the power of the notion of absolute truth as a weapon of domination is to be laid at the door of the notion itself. A dominant culture can employ the notion to oppress another only by claiming exclusive possession of the truth. Presumably, that claim must be given force by some kind of intellectual coercion (assuming the claim is not justified). But this coercion cannot itself work merely by a claim to possess the truth (on pain of regress). The real culprit, then, is the intellectual coercion applied and not the notion of truth itself. To be sure, if the notion of truth had no role except in such coercion, then it would have no more use than an assault rifle. But we have seen that the notion plays a number of roles having nothing to do with coercion of this sort. It plays epistemological roles that serve purposes quite internal to a culture and cannot have merely to do with one culture dominating another. And it plays explanatory roles that may well be indispensable to human life as we know it. This is not to say that the notion of truth in its epistemological roles cannot be employed for purposes of domination. Knowledge and true belief may be selectively ascribed and withheld in a way that reinforces stratification. Nor do I claim that there is any way to render the notion of truth useless for purposes of domination. Rather, I propose that the notion of truth belongs to the category of knives and other useful but sometimes lethal tools.

A final point here is that the domination objection to the notion of truth overlooks the possibility that the notion might be employed as a tool of liberation, to whatever extent it may be employed as a weapon of domination. Indeed, in as far as one opposes oppression by *arguing* against it, one must match a dominant culture's appeal to "truths" (such as the alleged superiority of that culture) with a countervailing appeal to truths. One must either debunk the claim to superiority or otherwise show that its truth is irrelevant to any entitlement to domination. The former effort involves arguing that the claim to superiority is not *true*. The latter effort also requires making claims about the relevance of truths and thus presupposes the possession of truth. Of course, one might attempt to oppose oppression without the use of argument. But even if it is possible to do so, why would one willingly relinquish the advantage of a tool effectively employed by the dominant culture?

In short, there would appear to be less to the worry that motivates recent complaints against truth than meets the eye. In any event, we can appreciate the force of that worry only in light of a full and accurate picture of the function that the notion of truth performs in human life. Once we see that the notion has key epistemological and explanatory roles to play, we are less likely to think of retiring it, or even to suppose that retirement is possible.

Notes

Chapter 2

1. Principle (M) may also be formulated as a principle about propositions rather than sentences: If <*p*> is identical with <*q*>, then <*p*> and <*q*> have the same truth-value. This version of (M) also generates an objection to relativism.

Chapter 3

1. I have said that the explanation I offer is contingent, but I really want to leave open the possibility that it is not just a contingent matter that true beliefs are generally necessary for useful behavior. For it might be that beliefs and actions have their content in virtue of the truth of the propositions believed. I do not want to rule out the possibility that wolf-avoidance behavior caused by the belief that the moon is made of cheese just could not count as the action of avoiding wolves. Again, I do not wish to rule out the possibility that a belief that standardly gave rise to wolf-avoidance behavior just could not count as the belief that the moon is made of cheese. But if actions and beliefs could not be like this, that would be because

the very conditions of content of beliefs and actions rule out their being like this. It would not, contrary to the pragmatic explanation, be because of anything in the nature of *truth*, at least nothing for which we need a pragmatic account of truth.

Chapter 4

1. Perhaps the best developed coherence theories of justification are those of BonJour 1985 and Lehrer 1990. It is notable that these authors explicitly reject the coherence theory of truth.

2. We may define justification-coherence in this way. A set of beliefs of a subject *S* justification-coheres for *S* just in case the set is consistent and exhibits certain relations of mutual support, such as deductive, inductive, probabilistic, and explanatory support. A proposition is then justification-coherent for a subject *S* just in case the proposition belongs to a set of propositions belief in which is justification-coherent for *S*.

3. It is worth considering here one last argument for a justification-condition theory of truth, the *manifestation* argument. This argument derives from the work of Michael Dummett (1978), though Dummett's writings are sufficiently elusive that I make no claim to have captured any of his arguments or views.

> (1) For any sentence or statement *S*, we can understand *S* only if we can manifest a knowledge of the conditions of meaning of *S*.
> (2) But the conditions of meaning of *S* are the truth-conditions of *S*.

(3) So we can manifest a knowledge of the conditions of meaning of *S* only if we can manifest a knowledge of the truth-conditions of *S*.
(4) But we can, for any sentence *S*, manifest a knowledge only of the *justification-conditions* of *S*. We could never manifest a knowledge of the truth-conditions of any sentence for which the truth-conditions diverged from the justification-conditions.
(5) So the truth-conditions of any sentence we can understand must be its justification-conditions.

Several premises of this argument could be questioned, but I will remark on premise (4) only. The premise assumes that we can always put ourselves in a position to believe a proposition expressed by a sentence we can understand if the proposition is justified. But even if justified belief is permissible belief, it does not follow that we can always believe or not believe *p* depending on whether $<p>$ is justified. It is certainly not *generally* true that we can always avoid doing what it is not permissible to do. For example, it is financially impermissible for me to stop paying my mortgage, even if I am unable to pay it (Feldman 1988, 240-243, Schmitt 1992, 94). In other words, it is not obvious that we are in any better position to manifest the justification-conditions of a proposition we understand than we are to manifest its truth-conditions when the latter are understood as diverging from the former. Thus, premise (4) is questionable. The manifestation argument rests on a dubious internalist epistemology.

Chapter 5

1. The two sentences are not, intuitively, equivalent. It should be noted, however, that the first sentence is in actuality false. But this does not hurt the objection, since the deflationist cannot admit that the first sentence is false. For on deflationism, this sentence is true. Moreover, even though the two sentences are both actually false, they are still not intuitively equivalent.

2. Additional interesting objections to deflationism appear in Boghossian 1989, Wright 1992, 231-236. Boghossian's objection is discussed by Wright.

Chapter 6

1. There is another ground on which it might be denied that explaining behavior requires ascribing content with truth-conditions. It might be claimed that all one need ascribe are beliefs and desires with *narrow* rather than wide content, and narrow content does not have truth-conditions. I would, however, contest both of these claims. See Stich (1983) for further discussion of narrow and wide content.

2. The idea of projecting beliefs and desires here bears some resemblance to the projectivism discussed in Chapter 1. Strictly speaking, however, it is not a version of projectivism about *beliefs* and *desires*. For projectivism about *x* entails that *x* does not exist, whereas on the present idea, projecting beliefs and desires is quite consistent with and indeed entails the reality of beliefs and desires. It entails it because projecting beliefs and desires is a matter of projecting one's *own* beliefs and desires or the beliefs and desires one would have in circumstances similar to those of the subject. The idea of projecting beliefs and desires may, however, be a version of projectivism about the

contents of beliefs and desires. Beliefs and desires have no contents taken in themselves. Their contents are always relative to an ascriber.

Conclusion

1. Yet another style of complaint, well developed by Stich (1991) is that, even on the correspondence theory, truth involves a relation to us, but the sort of relation it involves—a gerrymandered one—makes true belief an undesirable aim.

References

Alston, William P. (1989) *Epistemic Justification: Essays in the Theory of Knowledge*, Ithaca: Cornell University Press.

Aristotle (1968) *Metaphysics*, in *The Basic Works of Aristotle*, New York: Random House.

Austin, J. L. (1950) "Truth," *Proceedings of the Aristotelian Society*, supp. vol. 24: 111-128.

Ayer, A. J. (1936) *Language, Truth and Logic*, London: Victor Gollancz.

——— (1955) *The Foundations of Empirical Knowledge*, New York: St. Martin's.

Berkeley, George (1982) *A Treatise Concerning the Principles of Human Knowledge*, Indianapolis: Hackett.

Blackburn, Simon (1984) *Spreading the Word*, Oxford: Oxford University Press.

Blanshard, Brand (1941) *The Nature of Thought*, vol. 2, New York: Macmillan.

Boghossian, Paul (1989) "The Status of Content," *Philosophical Review*, 99: 157-183.

BonJour, Laurence (1985) *The Coherence Theory of Empirical Knowledge*, Cambridge, Mass.: Harvard University Press.

Brown, Robert, and C. D. Rollins, eds. (1969) *Contemporary Philosophy in Australia*, New York: Humanities Press.

Burnyeat, Miles (1976) "Protagoras and Self-refutation in Plato's *Theaetetus*," *Philosophical Review* 85: 172-195.
—— (1982) "Idealism and Greek Philosophy: What Descartes Saw and Berkeley Missed," *Philosophical Review* 91: 3-40.
Coady, C. A. J. (1992) *Testimony*, Oxford: Oxford University Press.
Craig, E. J. (1990) *Knowledge and the State of Nature*, Oxford: Oxford University Press.
Cummins, Robert (1989) *Meaning and Mental Representation*, Cambridge: MIT Press.
Davidson, Donald (1984a) *Inquiries into Truth and Interpretation*, New York: Oxford University Press.
—— (1984b) "Truth and Meaning," in Davidson (1984a).
—— (1984c) "Radical Interpretation," in Davidson (1984a).
Descartes, Rene (1985) *Meditations on First Philosophy*, in *The Philosophical Writings of Descartes*, trans. John Cottinghan, Robert Stoothoff, and Dugald Murdoch, Cambridge: Cambridge University Press.
Devitt, Michael (1981) *Designation*, New York: Columbia University Press.
—— (1984) *Realism and Truth*, Oxford: Basil Blackwell.
Devitt, Michael, and Kim Sterelny (1989) *Language and Reality: An Introduction to the Philosophy of Language*, Cambridge: MIT Press.
Dewey, John (1916) "What Pragmatism Means by 'Practical'" in *Essays in Experimental Logic*, Chicago: University of Chicago Press.
—— (1938) *Logic: The Theory of Inquiry*, New York: Holt.
Dummett, Michael (1978) *Truth and Other Enigmas*, Cambridge, Mass.: Harvard University Press.
Ellis, Brian (1969) "An Epistemological Concept of Truth," in Brown and Rolllins (1969).
Feldman, Richard (1988) "Epistemic Obligations," in Tomberlin (1988).

Field, Hartry (1972) "Tarski's Theory of Truth," *Journal of Philosophy* 69: 347-375.

——— (1986) "The Deflationary Conception of Truth," in MacDonald and Wright (1986).

Fine, Kit (1976) "Vagueness, Truth and Logic," *Synthese* 30: 265-300.

Frege, Gottlob (1960) "On Sense and Reference," in Geach and Black (1960).

Friedman, Michael (1979) "Truth and Confirmation," *Journal of Philosophy* 76: 361-382.

Geach, Peter, and Max Black, eds. (1960) *Translations from the Philosophical Writings of Gottlob Frege*, Oxford: Blackwell.

Goldman, A. I. (1986) *Epistemology and Cognition*, Cambridge, Mass.: Harvard University Press.

——— (1992) "In Defense of the Simulation Theory," *Mind and Language* 7: 104-119.

Groark, Leo (1990) *Greek Scepticism: Anti-Realist Trends in Ancient Thought*, Montreal: McGill-Queen's University Press.

Grover, Dorothy (1990) "Truth and Language-world Connections," *Journal of Philosophy* 87: 671-687.

Grover, Dorothy, Joe Camp, and Nuel Belnap (1975) "A Prosentential Theory of Truth," *Philosophical Studies* 27: 72-124.

Hollis, Martin, and Steven Lukes, eds. (1982) *Rationality and Relativism*, Cambridge: MIT Press.

Horwich, Paul (1990) *Truth*, Oxford: Basil Blackwell.

Hume, David (1990) *Treatise of Human Nature*, Oxford: Oxford University Press.

James, William (1907) *Pragmatism: A New Name for Some Old Ways of Thinking*, New York: Longmans, Green & Co.

——— (1909) *The Meaning of Truth*, Cambridge, Mass.: Harvard University Press.

Johnson, Lawrence E. (1992) *Focusing on Truth*, London: Routledge.

Kant, Immanuel (1965) *The Critique of Pure Reason*, New York: St. Martin's.
Kirkham, Richard (1992) *Theories of Truth: A Critical Introduction*, Cambridge: MIT Press.
Kuhn, Thomas (1962) *The Structure of Scientific Revolutions*, Chicago: University of Chicago Press.
Lehrer, Keith (1990) *Theory of Knowledge*, Boulder: Westview.
Leibniz, G. W. (1951) *The Monadology*, in *Leibniz Selections*, ed. Philip Wiener, New York: Charles Scribner's Sons.
Lovejoy, A. O. (1908) "The Thirteen Pragmatisms II," *Journal of Philosophy* 5: 29-39.
MacDonald, G., and C. Wright, eds. (1986) *Fact, Science and Morality: Essays on A. J. Ayer's Language Truth and Logic*, Oxford: Basil Blackwell.
McDowell, John (1984) "Wittgenstein on Following a Rule," *Synthese* 58: 325-363.
Misak, C. J. (1991) *Truth and the End of Inquiry*, Oxford: Clarendon.
Moore, G. E. (1953) *Some Main Problems in Philosophy*, London: Allen and Unwin.
Neely, W. (forthcoming) "Pragmatism and Truth," manuscript.
Newton-Smith, William (1982) "Relativism and the Possibility of Interpretation," in Hollis and Lukes (1982).
Nietzsche, Friedrich (1979) *On Truth and Lies in a Nonmoral Sense* in *Philosophy and Truth: Selections from Nietzsche's Notebooks of the Early 1870s*, trans. Daniel Brazeale, Atlantic Highlands, N.J.: Humanities Press.
O'Connor, D. J. (1975) *The Correspondence Theory of Truth*, London: Hutchinson.
Okrent, Mark (1993) "The Truth, the Whole Truth, and Nothing but the Truth," *Inquiry* 36: 381-404.
Peirce, C. S. (1931-1958) *Collected Papers of Charles Sanders Peirce*, vols. 1-8, ed. Charles Hartshorne and Paul Weiss (1-6) and Arthur Burks (7-8), Cambridge, Mass.: Harvard University Press.

Plato (1973a) *Sophist*, in *The Collected Dialogues of Plato*, ed. Edith Hamilton and Huntington Cairns, Princeton: Princeton University Press.

—— (1973b) *Theaetetus*, in *The Collected Dialogues of Plato*, ed. Edith Hamilton and Huntington Cairns, Princeton: Princeton University Press.

Pollock, John (1974) *Knowledge and Justification*, Princeton: Princeton University Press.

Price, Huw (1988) *Facts and the Value of Truth*, Oxford: Basil Blackwell.

Putnam, Hilary (1983) "Why Reason Can't Be Naturalized" in *Realism and Reason*, Cambridge: Cambridge University Press.

—— (1990) *Realism with a Human Face*, ed. James Conant, Cambridge, Mass.: Harvard University Press.

Quine, W. V. (1970) *Philosophy of Logic*, Englewood Cliffs, N.J.: Prentice-Hall.

Ramsey, F. P. (1927) "Facts and Propositions," *Proceedings of the Aristotelian Society*, supp. vol. 7: 153-170.

Rorty, Richard (1982) *Consequences of Pragmatism*, Minneapolis: University of Minnesota Press.

—— (1991) *Objectivity, Relativism and Truth*, Cambridge: Cambridge University Press.

Rouse, Joseph (1983) *Knowledge and Power: Toward a Political Philosophy of Science*, Ithaca, N.Y.: Cornell University Press.

Russell, Bertrand (1967) "Pragmatism" and "William James' Conception of Truth," in *Philosophical Essays*, New York: Simon and Schuster.

Sanford, David (1977) "Competing Semantics of Vagueness: Many Values Versus Super Truth," *Synthese* 33: 195-210.

Sapir, Edward (1949) *Selected Writings in Language, Culture and Personality*, ed. David G. Mandelbaum, Berkeley: University of California Press.

Schiffer, Stephen (1972) *Meaning*, Oxford: Oxford University Press.

Schmitt, Frederick (1992) *Knowledge and Belief*, London: Routledge.

———, ed. (1994a) *Socializing Epistemology: The Social Dimensions of Knowledge*, Lanham, Md.: Rowman and Littlefield.

——— (1994b) "Socializing Epistemology: An Introduction Through Two Sample Issues," in Schmitt (1994a).

——— (1994c) "The Justification of Group Belief," in Schmitt (1994a).

Spinoza, Baruch (1985) *Treatise on the Emendation of the Intellect and Ethics*, in *The Collected Works of Spinoza*, vol. 1, Princeton: Princeton University Press.

Stich, Stephen (1983) *From Folk Psychology to Cognitive Science: The Case Against Belief*, Cambridge: MIT Press.

——— (1991) *The Fragmentation of Reason*, Cambridge, Mass.: MIT Press.

Strawson, P. F. (1950) "Truth," *Proceedings of the Aristotelian Society*, supp. vol. 24: 129-156.

Stroud, Barry (1978) *Hume*, London: Routledge.

——— (1984) *The Significance of Philosophical Scepticism*, Oxford: Oxford University Press.

Tarski, Alfred (1956) "The Concept of Truth in Formalized Languages," in *Logic, Semantics and Metamathematics*, trans. J. H. Woodger, Oxford: Oxford University Press.

Tomberlin, James, ed. (1988) *Philosophical Perspectives* 2, *Epistemology*, Atascadero, Calif.: Ridgeview.

Vision, Gerald (1988) *Modern Anti-Realism and Manufactured Truth*, London: Routledge.

Walker, Ralph C. S. (1989) *The Coherence Theory of Truth*, London: Routledge.

Whewell, William (1989) *Novum Organon Renovatum*, Bk. 2, in *Theory of Scientific Method*, ed. R. E. Butts, Indianapolis: Hackett.

Whorf, Benjamin Lee (1956) *Language, Thought, and Reality*, ed. and intro. John B. Carroll, Cambridge: MIT Press.

Williams, Bernard (1978) *Descartes: The Project of Pure Enquiry*, New York: Penguin.

Williams, C. J. F. (1976) *What Is Truth?* Cambridge: Cambridge University Press.

Williams, Michael (1986) "Do We (Epistemologists) Need a Theory of Truth?" *Philosophical Topics* 14: 223-242.

Wittgenstein, Ludwig (1958) *Philosophical Investigations*, trans. G. E. M. Anscombe, 3rd ed., Oxford: Blackwell.

Wright, Crispin (1992) *Truth and Objectivity*, Cambridge, Mass.: Harvard University Press.

About the Book and Author

The concept of truth lies at the heart of philosophy; whether one approaches it from epistemology or metaphysics, or from the philosophy of language or the philosophy of science or religion, one must come to terms with the nature of truth.

In this brisk introduction, Frederick Schmitt covers all the most important historical and contemporary theories of truth. Along the way he also sheds considerable light on such closely related issues as realism and idealism, absolutism and relativism, and the nature of contemporary pragmatism.

In a time when it is fashionable for scholars outside of philosophy to deny the possibility of truth, Schmitt's lucid, technically accurate survey offers the easiest way to understand what is really at stake in such denials.

Truth: A Primer is a quick but accurate and philosophically sophisticated overview that will prove invaluable to philosophers and their students in a wide range of courses, in particular epistemology, metaphysics, and philosophy of language.

Frederick F. Schmitt is professor of philosophy at the University of Illinois at Urbana-Champaign. He is author of *Knowledge and Belief* and editor of *Socializing Epistemology* as well as author of many articles on knowledge, truth, and the history of epistemology.

Index